PRACTICAL GUIDE TO DATA STRUCTURES AND ALGORITHMS IN PYTHON

Master Problem-Solving with Efficient Algorithms

THOMPSON CARTER

TABLE OF CONTENTS

INTRODUCTION

"Practical Guide to Data Structures and Algorithms in Python"

In the rapidly evolving field of computer science, a solid grasp of data structures and algorithms is crucial for anyone aspiring to build efficient, scalable, and maintainable software solutions. "Practical Guide to Data Structures and Algorithms in Python" is designed to provide readers with an accessible, jargon-free guide to understanding these essential concepts using Python, one of the most popular and versatile programming languages today.

This book is aimed at readers who want to gain a deep understanding of data structures and algorithms while building practical skills to tackle real-world programming challenges. Whether you're a computer science student, a software developer, or a self-taught programmer, this guide offers a structured and detailed journey into the core principles and advanced techniques that will set you up for success in any coding environment.

Why Data Structures and Algorithms Matter

Imagine a well-organized toolbox. Inside, each tool has its purpose, and when used correctly, it makes the task at hand easier, more efficient, and often more enjoyable. Data structures and algorithms are like the tools in that toolbox: they allow programmers to approach problems methodically and find optimized solutions.

Data Structures organize, store, and manage data in a way that enables efficient access and modification. They are fundamental to solving problems that involve storing large amounts of data, manipulating complex information, or maintaining data integrity across large systems.

Algorithms are a set of well-defined instructions that help us solve a problem or perform a computation. Algorithms define the logical steps needed to transform input data into useful output. The choice of algorithms can impact the performance, reliability, and scalability of software, especially in applications where processing speed, memory usage, and resource constraints are critical.

Together, data structures and algorithms form the foundation of software design, powering everything from simple applications to complex systems like databases, operating systems, and even artificial intelligence. In fields like web development, data science, game design, and network engineering, the importance of these concepts cannot be overstated. By mastering them, programmers can develop more robust and flexible solutions, make efficient use of computational resources, and optimize program performance.

Why Python?

Python is an ideal language for learning data structures and algorithms for several reasons. Its syntax is clean and intuitive, which allows readers to focus on the underlying concepts without being distracted by complex syntax rules. Python's extensive library support, coupled with its readability and popularity across diverse programming communities, makes it a perfect choice for both beginners and experienced programmers.

Additionally, Python's versatile data types—such as lists, dictionaries, and sets—are particularly useful for implementing many foundational data structures and algorithms. Its built-in functions and modules, like heapq for heaps or collections for deques, simplify complex implementations. This book uses Python to demonstrate concepts because it allows readers to quickly transition from theoretical concepts to practical applications, enabling a smooth learning curve.

How This Book is Structured

This book is organized into chapters that follow a logical progression from basic concepts to more advanced techniques. Each chapter is designed to stand on its own, allowing readers to use this book as both a comprehensive guide and a reference.

1. **Foundational Concepts**: The opening chapters introduce the fundamentals of data structures, algorithms, and Python basics. Concepts like Big O notation, which helps in analyzing time and space complexity, are covered early on to provide a foundation for understanding the efficiency of different approaches.

2. **Basic Data Structures**: This section covers essential data structures such as arrays, lists, stacks, queues, and hash

tables. Each data structure is accompanied by clear explanations, real-world examples, and implementation details. Practical scenarios demonstrate when and why to use these structures.

3. **Trees and Graphs**: Trees and graphs are more complex data structures with a wide range of applications, from representing hierarchical data to modeling networks. Chapters on binary search trees, heaps, and graphs delve into their uses, traversal techniques, and implementations.

4. **Sorting and Searching Algorithms**: This section introduces sorting algorithms like merge sort and quicksort, as well as searching techniques such as linear and binary search. These algorithms are the backbone of many applications, including databases, search engines, and data processing pipelines.

5. **Advanced Data Structures**: Here, we explore data structures like tries and segment trees, which are invaluable in applications like text searching, autocompletion, and range queries. These data structures address specialized problems and are crucial in fields like natural language processing and competitive programming.

6. **Dynamic Programming and Greedy Algorithms**: Dynamic programming and greedy algorithms are essential for solving optimization problems. The chapters cover the principles behind these techniques and apply them to

classic problems, providing a systematic approach to tackling complex challenges efficiently.

7. **Problem-Solving Techniques and Interview Tips**: The final section focuses on applying the skills learned throughout the book. It offers a structured approach to problem-solving, practice problems that combine multiple structures and algorithms, and tips for succeeding in technical interviews.

Each chapter is packed with practical examples and step-by-step coding exercises in Python. Real-world applications are highlighted to demonstrate how the concepts are used in industry, helping readers bridge the gap between theory and practice.

How to Use This Book

This book is intended to be hands-on, with each chapter featuring examples and exercises. Here are some tips on how to get the most out of it:

- **Start with the Basics**: If you're new to data structures and algorithms, begin with the foundational chapters. Concepts like Big O notation and basic data types will be crucial as you progress to more advanced topics.
- **Code Along**: Whenever possible, try coding the examples yourself. This will reinforce your understanding and help you develop muscle memory for coding patterns.

- **Work Through the Exercises**: Each chapter includes exercises designed to challenge your understanding of the concepts. They range from straightforward questions to more complex problems that require critical thinking.

- **Experiment and Build**: Once you're comfortable with a data structure or algorithm, try applying it to a small project or a problem from an online coding platform. Experimenting with variations will deepen your understanding.

- **Refer Back to Previous Chapters**: Many concepts build upon each other. Don't hesitate to revisit earlier chapters if you encounter concepts that seem challenging.

Real-World Applications of Data Structures and Algorithms

To emphasize the practical side of this book, each chapter is filled with real-world applications of data structures and algorithms. Here are some examples:

1. **Social Networks and Graphs**: Graphs are used to model relationships in social networks, where nodes represent users and edges represent connections. By applying graph traversal algorithms, social media platforms can suggest friends, recommend content, and identify communities within the network.

2. **Search Engines and Tries**: Search engines and autocomplete systems use tries to efficiently store and

retrieve search terms and predictions. A trie enables fast retrieval of words with a common prefix, which is essential for autocomplete features, spell-checking, and text processing.

3. **E-commerce and Sorting Algorithms**: Online shopping platforms use sorting algorithms to display products by relevance, price, or popularity. Quick sort and merge sort play a significant role in efficiently sorting large datasets to improve user experience and recommendation accuracy.

4. **Dynamic Programming in Route Optimization**: Dynamic programming is widely used in logistics and route optimization. Delivery services apply these techniques to plan routes, minimize travel time, and maximize efficiency. Algorithms like Dijkstra's and Bellman-Ford are used to find the shortest path and calculate the quickest delivery routes.

5. **Machine Learning and Optimization**: Many machine learning algorithms involve optimization problems that require dynamic programming or greedy algorithms. Decision trees, for example, rely on efficient data structures and algorithms to evaluate the best feature splits, while gradient descent is used for minimizing cost functions.

Preparing for Coding Interviews

One of the motivations for learning data structures and algorithms is to excel in coding interviews. In today's competitive job market, most tech companies assess candidates through technical interviews that focus on problem-solving skills. This book provides the foundational knowledge and problem-solving techniques you need to confidently tackle coding challenges.

The chapter on interview tips goes beyond theory to help you approach interview questions strategically. By understanding how to structure your answers, break down problems, and communicate your thought process, you'll be able to demonstrate your coding proficiency and logical thinking skills.

The Journey Ahead

Mastering data structures and algorithms is a rewarding journey that opens up new possibilities in software development. This book is not just about memorizing techniques but about cultivating a deeper understanding of how to approach problems methodically, select the best tools, and adapt solutions to different scenarios. By the end, you'll have a comprehensive set of skills that will enable you to write cleaner, faster, and more efficient code.

This book equips you not only with knowledge but with the confidence to apply what you've learned in real-world situations. As you move through each chapter, you'll start to see patterns, recognize familiar problem types, and develop intuition for which techniques to apply in different contexts.

Whether you're preparing for a technical interview, working on a personal project, or just looking to improve your programming abilities, "Practical Guide to Data Structures and Algorithms in Python" is here to guide you every step of the way.

CHAPTER 1: INTRODUCTION TO DATA STRUCTURES AND ALGORITHMS

This introductory chapter sets the stage for understanding data structures and algorithms and prepares readers with the necessary Python setup for practical examples throughout the book.

Overview of Data Structures and Algorithms

1. **What Are Data Structures?**

    o   Data structures are organized ways of storing and organizing data to enable efficient access and modification. They're fundamental to programming, as they directly impact how quickly and effectively a program can handle data.

    o   Examples of data structures include arrays, lists, stacks, queues, linked lists, trees, and graphs.

2. **What Are Algorithms?**

    o   An algorithm is a step-by-step procedure for solving a problem or performing a task. It's a sequence of instructions that outline how to perform a calculation, manipulate data, or automate reasoning tasks.

- o Examples of algorithms range from simple tasks (like sorting a list) to complex problem-solving (like finding the shortest path in a network).

3. **The Relationship Between Data Structures and Algorithms**

   - o Data structures and algorithms work together to create efficient and effective programs. The choice of data structure can greatly impact the performance of an algorithm, making certain operations faster or slower.

   - o For instance, choosing the right data structure for storing data can make searching, inserting, and deleting elements significantly faster.

Why They're Essential in Programming

1. **Efficiency and Performance**

   - o In programming, efficiency is crucial, especially for tasks involving large datasets or complex computations. The right choice of data structure and algorithm can make the difference between a program that completes a task in seconds and one that takes hours.

   - o Algorithms are often evaluated based on their time complexity (how quickly they complete based on the input size) and space complexity (how much memory they require). Understanding these concepts helps in creating optimized solutions.

2. **Problem Solving and Software Design**

   o Data structures and algorithms aren't just about making code faster; they're about enabling you to solve problems effectively. For instance, using a queue data structure for task scheduling or a graph for mapping out networks simplifies complex problem-solving.

   o In software development, knowledge of these concepts allows developers to design scalable, maintainable, and high-performance applications.

3. **Essential for Interviews and Industry**

   o Data structures and algorithms are core topics in technical interviews, as they demonstrate a candidate's problem-solving skills and coding proficiency.

   o In industry, the ability to choose and implement appropriate data structures and algorithms is essential for tackling real-world engineering challenges, making these skills invaluable for career development.

Python Basics and Setup for the Book Examples

1. **Why Python?**

- o Python is a high-level, versatile programming language known for its readability, simplicity, and large collection of libraries. It's widely used in data science, web development, and scripting, making it an ideal language for this book.

- o Python's dynamic nature and built-in data structures (like lists, sets, and dictionaries) make it particularly well-suited for demonstrating data structures and algorithms.

2. **Setting Up Your Python Environment**

   - o **Installation**: Download and install Python from python.org. This book assumes Python 3.x, as Python 2 is no longer supported.

   - o **IDEs and Editors**: Recommended tools include Jupyter Notebook, PyCharm, or Visual Studio Code for writing and testing Python code. Each has features to help visualize code and track variables, which can aid in understanding algorithms.

   - o **Running Python Code**: Readers can run Python scripts in the terminal, or use interactive environments like Jupyter Notebook to run code snippets line-by-line, which is particularly helpful for learning.

3. **Python Basics Refresher**

- o **Data Types**: Basic types include integers, floats, strings, and booleans. Complex data types like lists, dictionaries, and sets will be covered in detail in later chapters.

- o **Control Structures**: Basic control structures like loops (for, while) and conditionals (if, else, elif) are essential for constructing algorithms.

- o **Functions and Modules**: Modular code is easier to maintain. Defining functions allows you to break down complex algorithms into manageable parts.

- o **Installing Libraries**: Some advanced data structures and algorithms require external libraries. To install them, use Python's package manager, pip, in the terminal:

  python
  pip install numpy

- o **Error Handling**: Understanding error handling with try, except, and finally statements helps in debugging code, especially when working with complex algorithms.

4. **Writing and Testing Code**

- o This book will use a "test-driven" approach to help readers verify their understanding. Writing small tests after each implementation will ensure code correctness.

- **Example Test Code**:

```python
def test_function():
    assert my_function(5) == 25, "Test failed for input 5"
    print("All tests passed!")


test_function()
```

This chapter lays the foundation for the rest of the book, introducing the reader to essential concepts, the Python setup, and coding practices. Each chapter from here on will build on these fundamentals, providing practical applications and real-world scenarios for each data structure and algorithm.

CHAPTER 2: BIG O NOTATION AND ALGORITHM ANALYSIS

In this chapter, readers will learn how to analyze the efficiency of their code using Big O notation, a mathematical concept that helps describe the performance of algorithms. By understanding time and space complexity, readers will gain insight into choosing more efficient solutions.

Simple Introduction to Time and Space Complexity

1. **What is Big O Notation?**
   - o Big O notation provides a way to express the performance of an algorithm based on the size of the input. It's a standard used to describe the upper bounds of an algorithm's running time or memory usage.
   - o Big O describes how an algorithm's runtime or space requirements grow as the input size increases.

By focusing on the growth rate, Big O notation allows developers to predict how an algorithm will scale.

2. **Time Complexity**

   o Time complexity describes the amount of time an algorithm takes to complete as the input size grows. It's expressed in terms of Big O notation (e.g., $O(n)$, $O(n^2)$), where:

      ▪ n is the size of the input.

      ▪ $O(1)$ represents constant time, where the operation doesn't depend on the input size.

      ▪ $O(n)$ represents linear time, where the time grows directly with the input size.

      ▪ $O(n^2)$, quadratic time, indicates that the time grows proportionally to the square of the input size.

   o Understanding time complexity helps in comparing algorithms and choosing the one that performs best for a given task.

3. **Space Complexity**

   o Space complexity refers to the amount of memory an algorithm needs to run, also expressed in Big O notation. It includes memory needed for the variables, data structures, and any additional memory allocated within the algorithm.

- Examples:
  - An algorithm with O(1) space complexity uses a constant amount of memory, regardless of input size.
  - An algorithm with O(n) space complexity uses memory proportional to the input size.
- Knowing space complexity is essential in memory-constrained environments, as it can impact performance, especially with large datasets.

How to Measure the Efficiency of Code

1. **Identify the Basic Operations**

- To analyze an algorithm's efficiency, start by identifying its basic operations (e.g., comparisons, assignments). These operations usually define the algorithm's time complexity.
- Example:

```python
def find_max(arr):
    max_val = arr[0]    # Assignment operation (constant time)
    for num in arr:
        if num > max_val:  # Comparison operation (linear time)
```

max_val = num   # Assignment operation (only when condition is met)

return max_val

- o In the example, the for loop runs once per element, so the time complexity is O(n).

2. Counting Steps

- o Analyzing code often involves counting the number of steps as a function of the input size. For instance, nested loops indicate O(n^2) time complexity, as each loop multiplies the operations based on the input size.

- o Example of nested loops:

```python
def pair_combinations(arr):
    for i in arr:
        for j in arr:
            print(i, j)
```

- o Here, each element in arr is paired with every other element, so the time complexity is O(n^2).

3. Understanding Common Big O Classes

- o **Constant Time - O(1):** Algorithms that run in constant time are the most efficient in terms of time complexity, as they complete in the same amount of time regardless of the input size.

o **Logarithmic Time - O(log n):** Often seen in algorithms that reduce the problem size by half at each step, such as binary search.

o **Linear Time - O(n):** Common in algorithms that need to process each element once, like finding the maximum value in a list.

o **Quadratic Time - O(n^2):** Often occurs in algorithms with nested loops; each element interacts with every other element.

o **Exponential Time - O(2^n):** Seen in algorithms where each input generates two recursive calls, like solving certain recursive problems (e.g., Fibonacci without memoization).

o **Factorial Time - O(n!):** Very rare and impractical for large inputs, as the time grows extremely fast with input size.

Real-World Examples of Performance in Python

1. **Linear Search - O(n) Example**

   o Suppose you want to search for a value in a list. The linear search algorithm checks each item one by one, so it has a time complexity of O(n).

   o Example:

python

```python
def linear_search(arr, target):
    for i in range(len(arr)):
        if arr[i] == target:
            return i
    return -1
```

2. Binary Search - O(log n) Example

o Binary search is efficient on sorted lists. It works by repeatedly dividing the search interval in half, reducing the problem size quickly.

o Example:

python

```python
def binary_search(arr, target):
    low, high = 0, len(arr) - 1
    while low <= high:
        mid = (low + high) // 2
        if arr[mid] == target:
            return mid
        elif arr[mid] < target:
            low = mid + 1
        else:
            high = mid - 1
    return -1
```

3. Sorting Algorithms - Different Complexities

- **Bubble Sort - O(n^2):** Bubble sort has a quadratic time complexity because it involves nested loops.

```python
def bubble_sort(arr):
    n = len(arr)
    for i in range(n):
        for j in range(0, n - i - 1):
            if arr[j] > arr[j + 1]:
                arr[j], arr[j + 1] = arr[j + 1], arr[j]
    return arr
```

- **Merge Sort - O(n log n):** Merge sort divides the array, sorts each half recursively, and then merges them. It's more efficient than bubble sort for large datasets.

```python
def merge_sort(arr):
    if len(arr) <= 1:
        return arr
    mid = len(arr) // 2
    left = merge_sort(arr[:mid])
    right = merge_sort(arr[mid:])
    return merge(left, right)
```

```
def merge(left, right):
    result = []
    while left and right:
        if left[0] <= right[0]:
            result.append(left.pop(0))
        else:
            result.append(right.pop(0))
    result.extend(left or right)
    return result
```

4. **Trade-offs Between Time and Space Complexity**

    o   Some algorithms are fast in terms of time but require more memory (e.g., merge sort), while others are slower but use minimal memory (e.g., bubble sort).

    o   It's important to understand these trade-offs when selecting an algorithm, especially in scenarios with limited memory or processing power.

In this chapter, we explored Big O notation and learned to measure the efficiency of algorithms in terms of time and space complexity. We discussed real-world performance examples in Python, covering algorithms with various complexities. By understanding these foundational concepts, readers can now assess and compare the efficiency of algorithms, equipping them to make informed decisions about which approach best fits a given problem.

In the next chapter, we'll dive into Python's built-in data types, providing a practical look at commonly used data structures and how they're implemented in Python.

Chapter 3: Python Built-in Data Types

This chapter introduces Python's core data types—lists, dictionaries, and sets. Each data type has unique properties and use cases, and understanding them will give readers a strong foundation for choosing the right tool for each problem.

Introduction to Python's Basic Data Types

Python offers a range of built-in data types that simplify data handling and manipulation. The most versatile data types include lists, dictionaries, and sets. Each has specific characteristics and is optimized for particular operations.

1. **Lists**
   - o Lists are ordered, mutable sequences that allow duplicate elements.

- o Lists can store any type of object, making them highly versatile. They support indexing and slicing, which allows direct access and modification of elements at specific positions.
- o Lists are implemented as dynamic arrays in Python, which means they can grow and shrink as needed.

2. **Dictionaries**

- o Dictionaries are unordered collections that store key-value pairs. They allow fast lookups, insertions, and deletions based on unique keys.
- o Each key in a dictionary is unique and immutable, while values can be mutable and of any data type.
- o Python's dictionaries are implemented as hash tables, providing average $O(1)$ time complexity for lookups.

3. **Sets**

- o Sets are unordered collections of unique elements, used to store and manage distinct items.
- o Sets do not allow duplicates and are implemented with hash tables, making operations like checking membership (in keyword) very fast.
- o Sets are mutable, allowing you to add or remove items. However, Python also provides frozenset, an immutable variant.

How They're Implemented and When to Use Them

Understanding when to use each data type depends on your specific needs:

1. **Lists**
   - Lists are the go-to data structure when you need to maintain order and allow duplicate values.
   - Ideal for situations where elements are accessed by position, such as creating queues, stacks, or maintaining ordered collections.
   - Common methods include:
     - .append(): Adds an element to the end of the list.
     - .pop(): Removes the last element or an element at a specific index.
     - .sort(): Sorts the list in place.
     - .index(): Finds the position of the first occurrence of a specified value.

2. **Dictionaries**
   - Use dictionaries when you need a collection of unique keys mapped to values, such as configurations, mappings, or associative arrays.
   - They are efficient for lookups and updates based on keys, with average O(1) complexity for these operations.
   - Common methods include:

- .get(): Retrieves a value for a given key; returns None if the key doesn't exist.
- .keys(): Returns all keys in the dictionary.
- .values(): Returns all values in the dictionary.
- .items(): Returns key-value pairs as tuples.

3. **Sets**

   o Sets are ideal for membership testing and situations where unique elements are required, like removing duplicates from a list or checking for common elements.

   o Use sets when order doesn't matter, and you need efficient membership checking.

   o Common methods include:

     - .add(): Adds an element to the set.
     - .remove(): Removes an element; raises an error if the element is not present.
     - .union(): Returns a new set with elements from the set and all others passed.
     - .intersection(): Returns a new set with common elements.

Example Applications in Small Scripts

Below are example use cases for each data type, highlighting their unique strengths.

1. **Example of Using Lists**

Use Case: Building a To-Do List App

- o Lists are perfect for maintaining an ordered collection of tasks. You can easily add, remove, or sort tasks by priority.

python
to_do_list = []

```
# Adding tasks
to_do_list.append("Buy groceries")
to_do_list.append("Finish homework")

# Removing a completed task
to_do_list.remove("Buy groceries")

# Accessing a task by index
print(to_do_list[0])  # Outputs: "Finish homework"
```

2. **Example of Using Dictionaries**

Use Case: Storing Product Prices in a Shop

- o A dictionary can be used to store product names as keys and their prices as values, making it easy to look up the price of a product or update it.

```python
product_prices = {
    "apple": 0.99,
    "banana": 0.49,
    "orange": 0.79
}

# Look up the price of a product
print("Price of apple:", product_prices.get("apple", "Not available"))

# Update the price of a product
product_prices["banana"] = 0.59

# Adding a new product
product_prices["grapes"] = 2.99
```

3. **Example of Using Sets**

   Use Case: Checking for Unique Visitors on a Website

   o Sets can be used to store unique visitor IDs to easily identify the total number of unique visitors to a website.

```python
visitor_ids = set()
```

```python
# Adding visitor IDs
visitor_ids.add("visitor1")
visitor_ids.add("visitor2")
visitor_ids.add("visitor1")  # Duplicate, will be ignored

# Checking if a specific visitor ID has been seen
if "visitor3" not in visitor_ids:
    print("New visitor")

# Printing total unique visitors
print("Total unique visitors:", len(visitor_ids))
```

4. Combining Data Types in an Application

Use Case: Building a Library Management System

- o Lists, dictionaries, and sets can be combined to manage a library's inventory and track users with checked-out books.

```python
python
library_inventory = [
    {"title": "Python 101", "author": "John Doe", "available": True},
    {"title": "Data Science Basics", "author": "Jane Smith", "available": True},
```

```
]

checked_out_books = set()
user_loans = {}  # Dictionary where key is user name, and
value is a list of books borrowed

# Borrowing a book
def borrow_book(user, book_title):
    for book in library_inventory:
        if book["title"] == book_title and book["available"]:
            book["available"] = False
            checked_out_books.add(book_title)
            if user in user_loans:
                user_loans[user].append(book_title)
            else:
                user_loans[user] = [book_title]
            print(f"{user} borrowed {book_title}")
            return
    print("Book not available")

borrow_book("Alice", "Python 101")
```

In this library example:

- A list of dictionaries, library_inventory, manages book information.

- A set, checked_out_books, keeps track of unique books that are currently checked out.
- A dictionary, user_loans, maps each user to the books they have borrowed.

In this chapter, we introduced Python's built-in data types—lists, dictionaries, and sets—and examined their unique characteristics, implementations, and practical applications. Understanding these data structures is essential for efficient and effective problem-solving in Python. With these foundational tools, readers are now prepared to start exploring more complex data structures in the following chapters.

Next, we'll dive into **arrays and lists**, focusing on their differences, use cases, and how they operate under the hood.

CHAPTER 4: ARRAYS AND LISTS

This chapter explores arrays and lists, two foundational data structures in programming. In Python, lists are highly versatile, but they differ from traditional arrays in several ways. Here, we'll dive into these differences, examine how Python lists work internally, and explore practical applications of lists, especially in data parsing.

Understanding Arrays and Lists: Dynamic vs. Static Arrays

1. **What are Arrays?**

   o An array is a collection of elements stored in contiguous memory locations, allowing constant-time access to elements by their index.

   o **Static Arrays**: These are fixed in size. Once created, you can't change their length. They are often used in languages like C and Java, where memory management is more manual.

o **Dynamic Arrays**: These arrays can grow or shrink in size as elements are added or removed. Python lists are implemented as dynamic arrays.

2. **Lists in Python as Dynamic Arrays**

o Python lists are dynamic, meaning they automatically adjust their size when you add or remove items. This feature is convenient but comes with a performance trade-off.

o Internally, Python lists allocate more memory than needed to allow for efficient appending. When the allocated memory is filled, the list will resize itself, typically doubling in size.

o The resizing operation has a cost ($O(n)$), but it's amortized, meaning that while a resize operation is costly, it doesn't happen frequently enough to impact the average performance ($O(1)$ for appending).

3. **Differences Between Arrays and Lists**

o **Flexibility**: Arrays require fixed types (all elements must be the same data type), while Python lists can store mixed data types.

o **Memory Efficiency**: Arrays are more memory-efficient because they store elements of a single type. Lists, on the other hand, are less memory-efficient but allow flexibility in storing various data types.

- o **Performance**: Static arrays offer predictable memory usage and constant-time access but lack flexibility. Dynamic arrays (like Python lists) provide flexibility with resizing but may incur occasional performance costs.

Python Lists and How They Work Internally

1. **Internal Representation of Python Lists**
   - o Python lists are essentially wrappers around C arrays, with additional memory allocation and management to support dynamic resizing.
   - o When you create a list, Python allocates more space than necessary. If more space is needed, Python increases the memory allocation in chunks rather than one item at a time.

2. **Memory Allocation and Resizing**
   - o Python's list resizing uses a strategy called "over-allocation," where it allocates more space than currently needed to reduce the number of times resizing must happen.
   - o When the list fills its allocated space, a new, larger block of memory is allocated, and all existing

elements are copied over (an O(n) operation). However, this doesn't happen with every append, so average append time is still O(1).

3. **Time Complexity of Common List Operations**

   o **Access by index (O(1))**: Python lists offer constant-time access to elements by index because they are stored in contiguous memory.

   o **Appending (O(1), amortized)**: Appending to the end of the list is efficient most of the time. Only occasionally will the list need to resize, which takes O(n) time but is amortized over many operations.

   o **Insertion and Deletion (O(n))**: Inserting or deleting elements at arbitrary positions is costly because elements need to be shifted.

Practical Usage of Lists in Applications Like Data Parsing

1. **Data Parsing and Processing**

   o Lists are commonly used for data parsing and handling data read from files or APIs, where the number of entries isn't known in advance. Their dynamic nature allows lists to grow as data is added.

   o Example: Parsing a CSV file and storing each row as a list of values.

   python

```
import csv

data = []
with open('data.csv', 'r') as file:
    reader = csv.reader(file)
    for row in reader:
        data.append(row)  # Each row is a list
```

2. **Storing and Manipulating Sequential Data**
   - Lists are ideal for storing sequences, such as sensor readings or daily temperatures. Lists allow easy access and modification of specific elements, and you can easily perform operations like slicing, filtering, and aggregating.

python
Copy code
```
temperatures = [72, 75, 78, 76, 73]
# Calculate average temperature
avg_temp = sum(temperatures) / len(temperatures)
```

3. **Lists for Buffering and Streaming Data**
   - Lists are effective for temporary data storage, such as buffering streams or storing logs before writing them to a file. You can dynamically append data as it arrives.

```python
python
logs = []

def log_event(event):
    logs.append(event)
    if len(logs) > 100:  # Flush logs to file when buffer is full
        with open('logs.txt', 'a') as file:
            for log in logs:
                file.write(log + '\n')
        logs.clear()
```

4. **Building Complex Data Structures with Lists**

   o   Lists can be used as building blocks for more complex data structures, such as stacks and queues.

   o   Example: Implementing a stack (Last In, First Out) using a list's append and pop methods.

```python
python
stack = []

def push(item):
    stack.append(item)

def pop():
    return stack.pop() if stack else None
```

```
push(1)
push(2)
print(pop())  # Output: 2
print(pop())  # Output: 1
```

5. **Using Lists with List Comprehensions**

   o Python list comprehensions allow for concise and efficient list creation and modification. This is especially useful in data transformation tasks.

```python
numbers = [1, 2, 3, 4, 5]
squares = [x ** 2 for x in numbers]  # Output: [1, 4, 9, 16, 25]
```

In this chapter, we explored the concepts of arrays and lists, understanding the differences between static and dynamic arrays. We dove into how Python lists are implemented internally as dynamic arrays with memory over-allocation strategies and discussed the average time complexities for common list operations. Finally, we looked at practical applications of lists in Python, including data parsing, buffering, and building basic data structures.

In the next chapter, we'll explore **stacks**, focusing on their Last In, First Out (LIFO) nature, practical uses, and how to implement them in Python.

CHAPTER 5: STACKS

This chapter introduces stacks, a fundamental data structure characterized by Last In, First Out (LIFO) behavior. We'll define stacks, explore real-world applications, implement a stack in Python, and solve some example problems that highlight its uses.

Definition and Real-World Applications

1. **What is a Stack?**
    o   A stack is a linear data structure that follows the Last In, First Out (LIFO) principle. This means that the last element added to the stack is the first one to be removed.
    o   Common operations on a stack include:

- **Push**: Add an element to the top of the stack.
- **Pop**: Remove the top element from the stack.
- **Peek**: Retrieve the top element without removing it.
- **IsEmpty**: Check if the stack is empty.

2. **Real-World Applications of Stacks**

   o **Browser History**: Web browsers use stacks to manage the back and forward functionality. Each time you navigate to a new page, it's pushed onto the history stack. Hitting "Back" pops the most recent page, returning you to the previous one.

   o **Undo Functionality in Text Editors**: Many text editors maintain an undo stack to reverse recent changes. Each change is pushed onto the stack, and when you hit "Undo," the most recent change is popped.

   o **Expression Evaluation**: Stacks are commonly used in expression evaluation and syntax parsing, such as evaluating mathematical expressions or checking for balanced parentheses.

   o **Function Call Stack**: In programming, function calls are managed via a call stack. Each function call pushes a frame onto the stack, and when the function completes, the frame is popped off, returning control to the caller.

Implementing a Stack in Python

Python does not have a built-in stack type, but lists and the deque module from collections can easily represent stacks.

1. **Implementing a Stack with Python List**

   Python lists can be used to implement a stack because they support append and pop operations efficiently.

   ```python
   class Stack:
       def __init__(self):
           self.items = []

       def push(self, item):
           self.items.append(item)

       def pop(self):
           return self.items.pop() if not self.is_empty() else None

       def peek(self):
           return self.items[-1] if not self.is_empty() else None

       def is_empty(self):
           return len(self.items) == 0
   ```

```python
def size(self):
    return len(self.items)

# Example usage
stack = Stack()
stack.push(10)
stack.push(20)
print(stack.pop())  # Outputs: 20
print(stack.peek())  # Outputs: 10
```

2. **Implementing a Stack with deque**

The deque class from Python's collections module is optimized for fast appends and pops and can be used as an alternative to lists for stack implementation.

python
```python
from collections import deque

class Stack:
    def __init__(self):
        self.items = deque()

    def push(self, item):
        self.items.append(item)
```

```python
def pop(self):
    return self.items.pop() if not self.is_empty() else None

def peek(self):
    return self.items[-1] if not self.is_empty() else None

def is_empty(self):
    return len(self.items) == 0

def size(self):
    return len(self.items)
```

```python
# Example usage
stack = Stack()
stack.push(10)
stack.push(20)
print(stack.pop())  # Outputs: 20
print(stack.peek())  # Outputs: 10
```

Example Problems That Utilize Stack Structures

1. **Problem 1: Balancing Parentheses**

   Stacks are commonly used to check if parentheses are balanced in expressions. Every time an opening parenthesis is encountered, it's pushed onto the stack. For every closing parenthesis, the stack is checked to see if there's a corresponding opening one.

python
Copy code

```python
def is_balanced(expression):
    stack = Stack()
    pairs = {')': '(', ']': '[', '}': '{'}

    for char in expression:
        if char in "({[":
            stack.push(char)
        elif char in ")}]":
            if stack.is_empty() or stack.pop() != pairs[char]:
                return False

    return stack.is_empty()


# Example usage
print(is_balanced("((a + b) * (c - d))"))  # Outputs: True
print(is_balanced("((a + b) * (c - d]"))   # Outputs: False
```

Explanation:

- o   Push each opening parenthesis onto the stack.

- o When encountering a closing parenthesis, pop the top of the stack. If it doesn't match the expected opening parenthesis, the expression is unbalanced.

2. **Problem 2: Reverse a String**

A stack can be used to reverse a string. By pushing each character onto the stack, we can then pop each character off in reverse order.

```python
def reverse_string(s):
    stack = Stack()
    for char in s:
        stack.push(char)
    reversed_str = "
    while not stack.is_empty():
        reversed_str += stack.pop()
    return reversed_str

# Example usage
print(reverse_string("hello"))  # Outputs: "olleh"
```

Explanation:

- o Each character is pushed onto the stack, storing it in LIFO order.
- o Popping each character builds the reversed string.

3. Problem 3: Evaluate Postfix Expressions

Postfix notation (Reverse Polish Notation) is a mathematical notation in which operators follow their operands. A stack is well-suited to evaluate postfix expressions since operators act on the most recent operands.

```python
def evaluate_postfix(expression):
    stack = Stack()
    for token in expression.split():
        if token.isdigit():
            stack.push(int(token))
        else:
            b = stack.pop()
            a = stack.pop()
            if token == '+':
                stack.push(a + b)
            elif token == '-':
                stack.push(a - b)
            elif token == '*':
                stack.push(a * b)
            elif token == '/':
                stack.push(a / b)
    return stack.pop()
```

```python
# Example usage
print(evaluate_postfix("3 4 + 2 * 7 /"))  # Outputs: 2.0
```

Explanation:

- For each number, push it onto the stack.
- For each operator, pop the top two numbers, apply the operator, and push the result back.
- The final result is obtained by popping the last remaining element.

4. **Problem 4: Browser Navigation (Back and Forward)**

This problem demonstrates how stacks can manage navigation history, using two stacks to store "back" and "forward" history.

```python
python
class BrowserHistory:
    def __init__(self):
        self.back_stack = Stack()
        self.forward_stack = Stack()

    def visit(self, url):
        if not self.back_stack.is_empty():
            self.forward_stack = Stack()   # Clear forward history
        self.back_stack.push(url)
```

```python
        print(f"Visited: {url}")

    def back(self):
        if self.back_stack.size() > 1:
            self.forward_stack.push(self.back_stack.pop())
            print(f"Back to: {self.back_stack.peek()}")

    def forward(self):
        if not self.forward_stack.is_empty():
            self.back_stack.push(self.forward_stack.pop())
            print(f"Forward to: {self.back_stack.peek()}")


# Example usage
browser = BrowserHistory()
browser.visit("google.com")
browser.visit("khanacademy.org")
browser.back()        # Outputs: Back to: google.com
browser.forward()                 # Outputs: Forward to:
khanacademy.org
```

Explanation:

- o Each visited page is pushed to the back_stack.
- o When "Back" is pressed, the current page is moved to forward_stack, and the previous page is displayed.
- o When "Forward" is pressed, a page is popped from forward_stack and added back to back_stack.

In this chapter, we explored stacks, a data structure that follows the Last In, First Out (LIFO) principle. We discussed various real-world applications, implemented a stack in Python, and solved problems that demonstrate its usefulness, including balancing parentheses, reversing strings, evaluating postfix expressions, and managing browser history. Understanding stacks provides a solid foundation for handling problems that require ordered, last-in-first-out data management.

In the next chapter, we'll dive into **queues**, a related structure with a First In, First Out (FIFO) principle, covering applications, implementations, and practical examples.

CHAPTER 6: QUEUES

This chapter introduces queues, a fundamental data structure that follows the First In, First Out (FIFO) principle. We'll cover the basics of queues, their types, and practical applications, along with Python implementations and examples of real-world usage.

Introduction to Queues and Where They're Used

1. **What is a Queue?**
   - A queue is a linear data structure that follows the First In, First Out (FIFO) principle, where the first element added is the first one removed.

- o Common operations on a queue include:
  - **Enqueue**: Add an element to the end of the queue.
  - **Dequeue**: Remove an element from the front of the queue.
  - **Peek**: Retrieve the front element without removing it.
  - **IsEmpty**: Check if the queue is empty.

2. **Real-World Applications of Queues**

   - o **Task Scheduling**: Operating systems and task schedulers use queues to manage processes, where the first task in line is the first to be processed.

   - o **Print Queue**: When sending documents to a printer, they're queued, allowing each document to print in the order it was submitted.

   - o **Customer Service**: Queues are used in customer service lines, ensuring that the first customer to arrive is served first.

   - o **Data Streaming**: Queues are used in data streaming (e.g., buffering video or audio) to handle incoming data in order.

Types of Queues

1. **FIFO Queue**

o The standard queue type, where elements are added at the end and removed from the front. It strictly follows FIFO order.

2. **Priority Queue**

o A priority queue is a type of queue where each element has a priority. Elements with higher priority are dequeued before elements with lower priority, regardless of their order of arrival.

o Priority queues are commonly used in scenarios where certain tasks or data need to be processed based on priority, such as emergency room triage or CPU process scheduling.

3. **Deque (Double-Ended Queue)**

o A deque allows elements to be added or removed from both ends (front and rear), making it more flexible than a standard FIFO queue.

o Deques are useful in applications like caching (e.g., LRU Cache) or scenarios where elements need to be processed from both ends.

Implementing Queues with Python

Python does not have a built-in queue type, but we can implement different types of queues using lists or the deque and PriorityQueue classes from the collections and queue modules.

1. **Implementing a Basic FIFO Queue with deque**

The deque class from the collections module is optimized for fast insertion and deletion from both ends, making it ideal for implementing a FIFO queue.

python
```python
from collections import deque

class Queue:
    def __init__(self):
        self.items = deque()

    def enqueue(self, item):
        self.items.append(item)

    def dequeue(self):
        return self.items.popleft() if not self.is_empty() else None

    def peek(self):
        return self.items[0] if not self.is_empty() else None

    def is_empty(self):
        return len(self.items) == 0

    def size(self):
        return len(self.items)
```

```python
# Example usage
queue = Queue()
queue.enqueue(10)
queue.enqueue(20)
print(queue.dequeue())  # Outputs: 10
print(queue.peek())     # Outputs: 20
```

2. Implementing a Priority Queue with PriorityQueue

Python's queue.PriorityQueue class provides a thread-safe implementation of a priority queue. It retrieves items based on their priority, with the smallest items dequeued first by default.

```python
python
from queue import PriorityQueue

class PriorityQueueWrapper:
    def __init__(self):
        self.queue = PriorityQueue()

    def enqueue(self, item, priority):
        self.queue.put((priority, item))  # Priority is the first
element in the tuple
```

```python
    def dequeue(self):
        return self.queue.get()[1] if not self.is_empty() else None

    def is_empty(self):
        return self.queue.empty()

# Example usage
priority_queue = PriorityQueueWrapper()
priority_queue.enqueue("task1", 2)
priority_queue.enqueue("task2", 1)    # Higher priority (lower number)
print(priority_queue.dequeue())    # Outputs: "task2"
```

3. Implementing a Deque with deque

The deque class supports both FIFO and LIFO operations, making it suitable for implementing a deque.

python
from collections import deque

```python
class Deque:
    def __init__(self):
        self.items = deque()
```

```python
    def add_front(self, item):
        self.items.appendleft(item)

    def add_rear(self, item):
        self.items.append(item)

    def remove_front(self):
        return self.items.popleft() if not self.is_empty() else None

    def remove_rear(self):
        return self.items.pop() if not self.is_empty() else None

    def is_empty(self):
        return len(self.items) == 0

    def size(self):
        return len(self.items)

# Example usage
deque_instance = Deque()
deque_instance.add_rear(10)
deque_instance.add_front(20)
print(deque_instance.remove_front())  # Outputs: 20
print(deque_instance.remove_rear())   # Outputs: 10
```

Real-World Examples Using Queues

1. **Example 1: Task Scheduling Simulation**

   This example simulates a basic task scheduling queue, where tasks are processed in the order they're added.

   python
   Copy code

```python
class TaskScheduler:
    def __init__(self):
        self.task_queue = Queue()

    def add_task(self, task):
        print(f"Adding task: {task}")
        self.task_queue.enqueue(task)

    def process_tasks(self):
        while not self.task_queue.is_empty():
            task = self.task_queue.dequeue()
            print(f"Processing task: {task}")

# Example usage
scheduler = TaskScheduler()
scheduler.add_task("Task 1")
scheduler.add_task("Task 2")
```

```
scheduler.process_tasks()
```

2. **Example 2: Handling Customer Service Queue**

This example demonstrates a basic customer service queue, where customers are served in the order they arrived.

python
Copy code

```python
class CustomerServiceQueue:
    def __init__(self):
        self.customers = Queue()

    def add_customer(self, customer_name):
        print(f"Customer {customer_name} joined the queue.")
        self.customers.enqueue(customer_name)

    def serve_customer(self):
        if not self.customers.is_empty():
            customer = self.customers.dequeue()
            print(f"Serving customer: {customer}")
        else:
            print("No customers to serve.")

# Example usage
```

```
service_queue = CustomerServiceQueue()
service_queue.add_customer("Alice")
service_queue.add_customer("Bob")
service_queue.serve_customer()    # Outputs: Serving customer: Alice
```

3. **Example 3: Priority Task Manager with Priority Queue**

In this example, we use a priority queue to manage tasks, where each task has a priority level. Higher-priority tasks (with lower numbers) are processed before lower-priority tasks.

python
```
class PriorityTaskManager:
    def __init__(self):
        self.priority_queue = PriorityQueueWrapper()

    def add_task(self, task, priority):
        print(f"Adding task: {task} with priority {priority}")
        self.priority_queue.enqueue(task, priority)

    def process_tasks(self):
        while not self.priority_queue.is_empty():
            task = self.priority_queue.dequeue()
            print(f"Processing task: {task}")
```

```python
# Example usage
manager = PriorityTaskManager()
manager.add_task("Clean database", 3)
manager.add_task("Fix urgent bug", 1)
manager.add_task("Send report", 2)
manager.process_tasks()
```

4. **Example 4: Implementing a Double-Ended Queue for Palindrome Checking**

This example demonstrates how to use a deque to check if a word is a palindrome by comparing characters from both ends.

```python
python
def is_palindrome(word):
    deque_instance = Deque()
    for char in word:
        deque_instance.add_rear(char)
    while deque_instance.size() > 1:
        if              deque_instance.remove_front()              !=
deque_instance.remove_rear():
            return False
    return True
```

```
# Example usage
print(is_palindrome("radar"))   # Outputs: True
print(is_palindrome("python"))   # Outputs: False
```

Explanation:

- o Characters are added to the deque from the rear.
- o Characters are removed from both ends simultaneously and compared, making it easy to check for symmetry.

In this chapter, we explored queues, a data structure that follows the First In, First Out (FIFO) principle. We covered different types of queues, including standard FIFO queues, priority queues, and double-ended queues (deques), and discussed their real-world applications. Using Python's deque and PriorityQueue classes, we implemented these queue types and worked through practical examples, such as task scheduling, customer service queues, priority task management, and palindrome checking.

In the next chapter, we'll examine **linked lists**, covering their structure, types, and practical uses, as well as implementing them in Python.

CHAPTER 7: LINKED LISTS

This chapter explores linked lists, a fundamental data structure that differs significantly from arrays and lists in terms of structure and use cases. Linked lists are particularly useful for scenarios where dynamic memory allocation and efficient insertions/deletions are needed. We'll discuss single and doubly linked lists, implement them in Python, and review real-world applications like undo features in text editors.

Concept of Linked Lists

1. **What is a Linked List?**

o A linked list is a linear data structure where elements, known as "nodes," are stored in a sequence. Each node contains:

  ▪ **Data**: The value or content of the node.

  ▪ **Pointer**: A reference (or link) to the next node in the sequence.

o Linked lists are dynamically sized, meaning they can grow or shrink as needed, unlike arrays, which have a fixed size.

2. **Types of Linked Lists**

o **Singly Linked List**: Each node points only to the next node in the sequence. It allows traversal in a single direction (forward).

o **Doubly Linked List**: Each node has two pointers— one pointing to the next node and another pointing to the previous node. This allows traversal in both directions (forward and backward).

o **Circular Linked List**: In a circular linked list, the last node points back to the first node, creating a circular structure. Circular linked lists can be singly or doubly linked.

Creating Linked Lists in Python

Python doesn't have a built-in linked list data type, so we can implement linked lists by defining custom classes.

1. **Singly Linked List Implementation**

A singly linked list has nodes where each node points to the next node. Below, we'll define a Node class to represent each node and a SinglyLinkedList class to manage the list.

```python
class Node:
    def __init__(self, data):
        self.data = data
        self.next = None


class SinglyLinkedList:
    def __init__(self):
        self.head = None

    def append(self, data):
        new_node = Node(data)
        if not self.head:
            self.head = new_node
        else:
            current = self.head
            while current.next:
                current = current.next
            current.next = new_node
```

```python
def display(self):
    nodes = []
    current = self.head
    while current:
        nodes.append(current.data)
        current = current.next
    print(" -> ".join(map(str, nodes)))


def delete(self, data):
    current = self.head
    if current and current.data == data:
        self.head = current.next
        return
    previous = None
    while current and current.data != data:
        previous = current
        current = current.next
    if current:
        previous.next = current.next


# Example usage
linked_list = SinglyLinkedList()
linked_list.append(1)
linked_list.append(2)
linked_list.append(3)
```

```
linked_list.display()  # Outputs: 1 -> 2 -> 3
linked_list.delete(2)
linked_list.display()  # Outputs: 1 -> 3
```

Explanation:

- o Each node in the linked list contains data and a pointer to the next node.
- o The append method adds a new node at the end of the list.
- o The delete method removes a node with a specified value from the list.

2. **Doubly Linked List Implementation**

In a doubly linked list, each node has two pointers: one to the next node and one to the previous node. This allows traversal in both directions.

python
```python
class DoublyNode:
    def __init__(self, data):
        self.data = data
        self.next = None
        self.prev = None


class DoublyLinkedList:
    def __init__(self):
```

```python
        self.head = None

    def append(self, data):
        new_node = DoublyNode(data)
        if not self.head:
            self.head = new_node
        else:
            current = self.head
            while current.next:
                current = current.next
            current.next = new_node
            new_node.prev = current

    def display_forward(self):
        nodes = []
        current = self.head
        while current:
            nodes.append(current.data)
            current = current.next
        print(" -> ".join(map(str, nodes)))

    def display_backward(self):
        nodes = []
        current = self.head
        while current and current.next:
```

```python
            current = current.next
        while current:
            nodes.append(current.data)
            current = current.prev
        print(" <- ".join(map(str, nodes)))


    def delete(self, data):
        current = self.head
        while current:
            if current.data == data:
                if current.prev:
                    current.prev.next = current.next
                if current.next:
                    current.next.prev = current.prev
                if current == self.head:   # Adjust head if
necessary
                    self.head = current.next
                return
            current = current.next


# Example usage
doubly_linked_list = DoublyLinkedList()
doubly_linked_list.append(1)
doubly_linked_list.append(2)
doubly_linked_list.append(3)
```

doubly_linked_list.display_forward()   # Outputs: 1 -> 2 -> 3

doubly_linked_list.display_backward()   # Outputs: 3 <- 2 <- 1

doubly_linked_list.delete(2)

doubly_linked_list.display_forward()   # Outputs: 1 -> 3

Explanation:

- o Each DoublyNode has pointers to both the next and previous nodes.
- o The display_forward method traverses from head to tail, while display_backward traverses from tail to head.
- o The delete method removes a specified node, adjusting links as necessary.

Real-World Applications of Linked Lists

1. **Undo/Redo Functionality in Text Editors**
   - o Linked lists, especially doubly linked lists, are used in text editors to implement the undo and redo features. Each change in the document is a node in the linked list, with pointers to the previous and next changes.

o   When a user presses "Undo," the editor can traverse backward to the previous change. When "Redo" is pressed, it moves forward.

2. **Browser Navigation (Back and Forward)**

o   Similar to undo/redo, linked lists can manage browser navigation history. Each visited page is a node in the list, allowing users to move back or forward through history.

3. **Image Viewer (Forward and Backward Navigation)**

o   Linked lists can be used in image viewers to navigate between images. Each image is represented by a node, with pointers to the next and previous images.

4. **Music Playlist Management**

o   Playlists often need to play songs in a specific order, with the ability to go to the previous or next song. Doubly linked lists are ideal for this as they allow efficient traversal in both directions.

In this chapter, we explored linked lists, a data structure where each element is connected by pointers. We discussed singly and doubly linked lists, learned how to implement them in Python, and explored real-world applications such as undo/redo functionality in text editors. Understanding linked lists gives insight into managing dynamic data structures, especially when flexible insertions and deletions are needed.

In the next chapter, we'll dive into **hash tables**, covering their unique properties, applications, and how they provide efficient data access in Python.

CHAPTER 8: HASH TABLES (DICTIONARIES)

Hash tables are a critical data structure in programming that provide efficient data retrieval. Python's implementation of hash tables, known as dictionaries, is highly optimized and widely used. In this chapter, we'll explore how hash tables work, examine hash functions and collision resolution strategies, and discuss real-world applications.

How Hash Tables Work and When to Use Them

1. **What is a Hash Table?**
   - A hash table is a data structure that stores key-value pairs. It uses a hash function to convert a key into an index, which determines where the value is stored in memory.
   - Hash tables offer very efficient lookups, insertions, and deletions, with average time complexity of O(1). This efficiency is due to the direct access provided by the hash function.

2. **Hash Tables in Python: Dictionaries**
   - Python's dict type is a hash table implementation. Each key-value pair is stored at an index determined by a hash of the key.
   - Dictionaries in Python are unordered collections, although in recent versions they maintain insertion order.
   - Example of a Python dictionary:

   python
   phone_book = {
       "Alice": "555-1234",

```
"Bob": "555-5678",

"Charlie": "555-8765"

}

print(phone_book["Alice"])  # Outputs: 555-1234
```

3. **When to Use Hash Tables**
   - Hash tables are ideal when you need:
     - **Fast Data Retrieval**: If you frequently need to retrieve values based on a unique key (like looking up a phone number by name), hash tables are optimal.
     - **Flexible Keys**: Unlike arrays, which use integer indices, hash tables can use various data types (like strings, tuples, etc.) as keys.
     - **Dynamic Size**: Hash tables grow as needed, making them suitable for dynamic data storage without needing a fixed size.

Hash Functions and Collision Resolution

1. **Hash Functions**
   - A hash function takes an input (key) and returns an integer (hash code), which is then used to find an index for the key in the hash table.
   - A good hash function distributes keys evenly across the hash table, reducing the likelihood of collisions.

2. **Collisions and Collision Resolution**
   - **What is a Collision?**: A collision occurs when two keys produce the same hash code and are assigned the same index in the hash table.
   - **Collision Resolution Strategies**:
     - **Chaining**: In chaining, each index in the hash table points to a list (or linked list) of entries that hash to the same index. When a collision occurs, the new key-value pair is added to the list at that index.
     - **Open Addressing**: In open addressing, if a collision occurs, the algorithm searches for the next available slot according to a probing sequence (e.g., linear probing, quadratic probing, or double hashing).
   - **Python's Approach**: Python dictionaries use open addressing with a variation of double hashing to resolve collisions, which helps maintain performance.

Example of a Hash Function with Simple Modulo Operation:

python
```python
def simple_hash(key, table_size):
    return hash(key) % table_size
```

```
# Assuming table_size is 10
print(simple_hash("Alice", 10))  # Outputs an index based
on Alice's hash code
```

Real-World Applications of Hash Tables

1. **Fast Data Retrieval in Databases**
   - Many databases use hash tables to manage indexing, allowing for quick lookups of data. For example, in a database table with a "user ID" field, a hash table index allows the database to rapidly locate a specific user's information.
   - Hash tables are also commonly used in in-memory databases (e.g., Redis) for storing and retrieving key-value pairs at high speed.

2. **Caching and Memoization**
   - Hash tables are essential in caching systems, where frequently accessed data is stored for quick retrieval. By using a hash table, caches can retrieve data in constant time.
   - In programming, memoization (caching results of function calls) often relies on hash tables to store computed results and avoid redundant calculations.

python

```python
# Example of memoization using a dictionary
fib_cache = {}

def fibonacci(n):
    if n in fib_cache:
        return fib_cache[n]
    if n <= 1:
        return n
    fib_cache[n] = fibonacci(n - 1) + fibonacci(n - 2)
    return fib_cache[n]

print(fibonacci(10))  # Outputs: 55
```

3. **Counting Frequency of Elements**
   - o Hash tables are perfect for counting occurrences, such as counting the frequency of words in a document or items in a list.
   - o Example: Counting word frequency using a dictionary.

```python
python
def count_words(text):
    word_count = {}
    words = text.split()
    for word in words:
        word_count[word] = word_count.get(word, 0) + 1
```

```
    return word_count
```

```
print(count_words("to be or not to be"))  # Outputs: {'to': 2,
'be': 2, 'or': 1, 'not': 1}
```

4. **Implementing Sets**

   o Sets are a collection of unique items and are often implemented as hash tables. Python's set type is built on a hash table, allowing for efficient membership tests (in keyword) and set operations (e.g., union, intersection).

python
```python
unique_items = set(["apple", "banana", "apple", "orange"])
print(unique_items) # Outputs: {'apple', 'banana', 'orange'}
```

5. **Data Deduplication**

   o Hash tables are often used to remove duplicates in large datasets. By inserting each item into a hash table and checking for membership, duplicates can be detected and ignored.

python
```python
def remove_duplicates(items):
    unique_items = {}
    for item in items:
        unique_items[item] = True
```

```
    return list(unique_items.keys())
```

```
print(remove_duplicates(["apple",    "banana",    "apple",
"orange"]))  # Outputs: ['apple', 'banana', 'orange']
```

6. **Symbol Table in Compilers**
   o Hash tables are used to implement symbol tables in compilers. A symbol table stores information about variables, functions, and other identifiers in a program, allowing the compiler to quickly look up identifiers and their associated information.

In this chapter, we explored hash tables and their implementation in Python through dictionaries. We discussed how hash tables use hash functions to quickly locate key-value pairs, examined collision resolution strategies like chaining and open addressing, and reviewed real-world applications such as fast data retrieval, caching, and counting element frequency. Hash tables are essential for scenarios where rapid access to data is required, and understanding them will help in building efficient applications.

In the next chapter, we'll dive into **trees**, introducing tree structures and covering basic types, including binary trees, along with their use cases and implementations in Python.

CHAPTER 9: TREES - BASICS

Trees are a powerful and versatile data structure with various applications in programming. In this chapter, we'll introduce trees and their properties, explore different types of trees, implement a basic tree in Python, and discuss real-world use cases like file system structures.

Introduction to Trees and Their Properties

1. **What is a Tree?**

- o A tree is a hierarchical, non-linear data structure composed of nodes. It starts from a **root** node and branches out into child nodes, resembling an upside-down tree in nature.
- o **Nodes**: Each node contains data and may have links to other nodes (children).
- o **Root**: The top-most node in a tree, with no parent.
- o **Leaf Nodes**: Nodes with no children, representing the ends of paths.
- o **Internal Nodes**: Nodes with at least one child.
- o **Edges**: Links between nodes.
- o **Height**: The longest path from the root to a leaf node.
- o **Depth**: The distance (number of edges) from the root to a given node.

2. **Key Properties of Trees**

- o Trees have a hierarchical structure, making them ideal for representing hierarchical data.
- o Each child node has only one parent, but each parent node can have multiple children.
- o Trees have various types and structures optimized for different applications (e.g., binary trees, AVL trees, B-trees).

3. **Why Use Trees?**

- Trees efficiently represent hierarchical data and relationships, such as organizational structures or file systems.
- Operations like searching, inserting, and deleting can be performed efficiently in balanced trees.

Different Types of Trees and Basic Implementations in Python

1. **Binary Tree**
   - A binary tree is a type of tree where each node has at most two children (typically called the left and right child).
   - Binary trees are commonly used for search and sorting operations, and they form the basis of many other types of trees.

python
```
class Node:
    def __init__(self, data):
        self.data = data
        self.left = None
        self.right = None


class BinaryTree:
    def __init__(self, root_data):
        self.root = Node(root_data)
```

```python
def insert_left(self, current_node, new_data):
    if current_node.left is None:
        current_node.left = Node(new_data)
    else:
        new_node = Node(new_data)
        new_node.left = current_node.left
        current_node.left = new_node


def insert_right(self, current_node, new_data):
    if current_node.right is None:
        current_node.right = Node(new_data)
    else:
        new_node = Node(new_data)
        new_node.right = current_node.right
        current_node.right = new_node
```

2. **Binary Search Tree (BST)**
   - o A binary search tree (BST) is a binary tree where each node's left child has a smaller value, and the right child has a larger value.
   - o This property makes BSTs efficient for search operations ($O(\log n)$ on average for balanced trees).

python
class BSTNode:

```python
def __init__(self, data):
    self.data = data
    self.left = None
    self.right = None

def insert(self, data):
    if data < self.data:
        if self.left is None:
            self.left = BSTNode(data)
        else:
            self.left.insert(data)
    else:
        if self.right is None:
            self.right = BSTNode(data)
        else:
            self.right.insert(data)

def find(self, data):
    if data < self.data:
        return self.left.find(data) if self.left else None
    elif data > self.data:
        return self.right.find(data) if self.right else None
    else:
        return self
```

3. AVL Tree

- o An AVL tree is a self-balancing binary search tree. It maintains a balance factor to ensure that no subtree is taller than another by more than one level.
- o When an imbalance occurs after insertion or deletion, AVL trees perform rotations to restore balance, keeping search operations efficient.

4. **B-Tree**

- o A B-tree is a balanced search tree optimized for disk storage. Each node in a B-tree can have multiple children, making it well-suited for large databases and file systems.

5. **Trie (Prefix Tree)**

- o A trie is a tree used to store a dynamic set of strings, where each node represents a character. It's commonly used for tasks like autocomplete and spell-checking, as it efficiently handles prefix-based search.

6. **Heap (Binary Heap)**

- o A binary heap is a complete binary tree used primarily as a priority queue. There are two types:
    - **Min-Heap**: The root node has the minimum value.
    - **Max-Heap**: The root node has the maximum value.

Use Cases of Trees in File System Structures

1. **File System Hierarchies**
   o File systems are naturally organized as trees, where folders represent nodes, and each folder can have multiple subfolders or files as children.
   o A root folder serves as the starting point (root node), with files and subfolders forming a tree-like structure below it.

Example: Simulating a Simple File System Tree

python
```
class FileNode:
    def __init__(self, name, is_file=False):
        self.name = name
        self.is_file = is_file
        self.children = []

    def add_child(self, child_node):
        self.children.append(child_node)

# Creating the file system structure
root = FileNode("root")
folder1 = FileNode("folder1")
folder2 = FileNode("folder2")
file1 = FileNode("file1.txt", is_file=True)
file2 = FileNode("file2.txt", is_file=True)
```

```
# Building the tree
root.add_child(folder1)
root.add_child(folder2)
folder1.add_child(file1)
folder2.add_child(file2)
```

2. **Database Indexing**
   - o Trees, particularly B-trees and B+ trees, are used to implement indexing in databases. They ensure efficient access to data, even with large datasets, by organizing records in a sorted, hierarchical manner.

3. **Autocomplete Systems**
   - o Tries (prefix trees) are used in autocomplete systems to store a large number of words and support efficient prefix-based searching, enabling fast word completions as users type.

4. **Network Routing**
   - o Trees, especially binary tries and prefix-based trees, are used in network routing to manage IP address hierarchies and ensure efficient packet routing.

5. **HTML Document Object Model (DOM)**
   - o HTML documents are represented as a tree structure (DOM tree) in web browsers, where each HTML element is a node. This structure allows

efficient traversal, manipulation, and rendering of web pages.

In this chapter, we explored trees and their properties, examined various types of trees, and implemented a basic binary tree and binary search tree in Python. We discussed real-world use cases such as file system structures, database indexing, and autocomplete systems, all of which leverage the hierarchical structure of trees for efficiency and scalability.

In the next chapter, we'll explore **binary search trees (BSTs)** in greater detail, covering insertion, deletion, and traversal techniques, along with their applications in searching and sorting.

CHAPTER 10: BINARY SEARCH TREES (BSTs)

Binary Search Trees (BSTs) are a specific type of binary tree that allow efficient data searching, insertion, and deletion. In this chapter, we'll define BSTs, implement insertion, deletion, and traversal algorithms, and explore their applications, particularly in search optimization.

Understanding Binary Trees and Binary Search Trees (BSTs)

1. **What is a Binary Tree?**
   - A binary tree is a hierarchical structure where each node has at most two children: a left child and a right child.
   - Binary trees provide the foundation for several specialized tree structures, including binary search trees.
2. **What is a Binary Search Tree (BST)?**
   - A binary search tree is a binary tree with an additional property: for any node in the tree:
     - All nodes in its left subtree contain values less than the node's value.
     - All nodes in its right subtree contain values greater than the node's value.
   - This structure allows for efficient searching, insertion, and deletion, as the BST property enables the tree to eliminate half of the nodes in each step of a search.
3. **BST Properties and Benefits**
   - BSTs provide an average time complexity of O(log n) for search, insertion, and deletion in balanced trees.
   - They're highly useful for ordered data and enable efficient in-order traversal to retrieve data in a sorted manner.

BST Insertion, Deletion, and Traversal Algorithms

1. **Insertion in a BST**
   - To insert a new node in a BST:
     1. Start from the root.

2. Compare the new value with the current node's value.
3. If the new value is smaller, move to the left child; if it's larger, move to the right child.
4. Repeat this process until you find an empty spot, and insert the new node there.

Python Code for BST Insertion:

```python
class BSTNode:
    def __init__(self, data):
        self.data = data
        self.left = None
        self.right = None

    def insert(self, data):
        if data < self.data:
            if self.left is None:
                self.left = BSTNode(data)
            else:
                self.left.insert(data)
        else:
            if self.right is None:
                self.right = BSTNode(data)
            else:
                self.right.insert(data)

# Example usage
root = BSTNode(10)
root.insert(5)
root.insert(15)
root.insert(7)
```

2. **Deletion in a BST**
   o To delete a node in a BST, there are three main cases to consider:

- **Node with No Children** (Leaf Node): Simply remove the node.
- **Node with One Child**: Replace the node with its child.
- **Node with Two Children**: Find the node's in-order successor (the smallest node in its right subtree), replace the node's value with the successor's value, and delete the successor node.

Python Code for BST Deletion:

```python
def delete(self, data):
    if data < self.data:
        if self.left:
            self.left = self.left.delete(data)
    elif data > self.data:
        if self.right:
            self.right = self.right.delete(data)
    else:  # Node to be deleted found
        # Case 1: Node with no children
        if not self.left and not self.right:
            return None
        # Case 2: Node with one child
        if not self.left:
            return self.right
        if not self.right:
            return self.left
        # Case 3: Node with two children
        min_larger_node = self.right.find_min()
        self.data = min_larger_node.data
        self.right = self.right.delete(min_larger_node.data)
    return self

def find_min(self):
    current = self
```

```
while current.left:
    current = current.left
return current
```

3. **BST Traversal Algorithms**
   o BST traversal methods allow us to visit each node in a specified order. Common traversal techniques include:
     - **In-order Traversal (Left, Root, Right)**: Visits nodes in ascending order for a BST.
     - **Pre-order Traversal (Root, Left, Right)**: Visits each node before its children, commonly used for tree copying.
     - **Post-order Traversal (Left, Right, Root)**: Visits children before their parent, useful for tree deletion.

Python Code for In-order Traversal:

```python
def in_order_traversal(self):
    elements = []
    if self.left:
        elements += self.left.in_order_traversal()
    elements.append(self.data)
    if self.right:
        elements += self.right.in_order_traversal()
    return elements

# Example usage
root = BSTNode(10)
root.insert(5)
root.insert(15)
root.insert(7)
print(root.in_order_traversal())  # Outputs: [5, 7, 10, 15]
```

Applications of BSTs in Search Optimization

1. **Efficient Searching**
   - A BST enables efficient searching by allowing you to eliminate half of the remaining nodes at each step (similar to binary search).
   - Searching for a value in a balanced BST has an average time complexity of O(log n), which is significantly faster than O(n) for linear search on an unsorted list.

2. **Dynamic Sorting**
   - A BST can be used to maintain sorted data dynamically, allowing efficient insertion while preserving order. In-order traversal of a BST retrieves the elements in sorted order.

3. **Database Indexing**
   - Balanced BSTs are sometimes used in database indexing to speed up searches. While balanced BSTs (like AVL or Red-Black Trees) maintain order, B-Trees and B+ Trees are often used in larger databases for efficient indexing with minimal re-balancing.

4. **Autocomplete and Lexicographical Data**
   - BSTs can be used in conjunction with tries to build efficient autocomplete systems. By storing each word as a sequence of characters in lexicographical order, search queries for suggestions can be completed efficiently.

5. **Binary Search Implementation**
   - BSTs inherently support binary search operations, where you compare the target value with the current node and move either left or right, depending on whether the target is smaller or larger than the node's value.

Python Code for Binary Search in a BST:

```python
def search(self, data):
```

```
if data < self.data:
    return self.left.search(data) if self.left else None
elif data > self.data:
    return self.right.search(data) if self.right else None
else:
    return self  # Data found

# Example usage
root = BSTNode(10)
root.insert(5)
root.insert(15)
root.insert(7)
result = root.search(7)
if result:
    print("Data found:", result.data)  # Outputs: Data found:
7
else:
    print("Data not found")
```

In this chapter, we explored binary search trees (BSTs), which are binary trees with an ordering property that enables efficient search, insertion, and deletion operations. We implemented BSTs in Python, covering insertion, deletion, and traversal methods, and discussed their applications in search optimization, such as dynamic sorting, database indexing, and binary search. BSTs provide a foundation for understanding more complex search trees, like AVL trees and B-Trees, used in various high-performance applications.

In the next chapter, we'll discuss **heaps and priority queues**, which allow efficient retrieval of the minimum or maximum element, and cover their implementations and applications.

CHAPTER 11: HEAPS AND PRIORITY QUEUES

Heaps are specialized binary trees that support efficient retrieval of the minimum or maximum element, making them ideal for implementing priority queues. In this chapter, we'll define heaps, explore how priority queues work, examine max-heaps and min-heaps, and implement them using Python's heapq library and custom code.

What is a Heap and How Priority Queues Work

1. **What is a Heap?**

   o A heap is a binary tree with two main properties:

     ▪ **Complete Tree**: All levels of the tree are fully filled except possibly the last, which is filled from left to right.

     ▪ **Heap Property**:

       ▪ In a **min-heap**, each parent node's value is less than or equal to the values of its children. The minimum value is always at the root.

       ▪ In a **max-heap**, each parent node's value is greater than or equal to the values of its children. The maximum value is always at the root.

2. **What is a Priority Queue?**

- A priority queue is a data structure where elements are processed based on their priority rather than just the order they were added.
- Priority queues can be implemented using heaps, where:
  - A min-heap retrieves the element with the lowest priority.
  - A max-heap retrieves the element with the highest priority.

3. Why Use Heaps and Priority Queues?

- Heaps allow efficient access to the minimum or maximum element, with operations like insertion, deletion, and retrieval taking $O(\log n)$ time.
- Priority queues are commonly used in scheduling systems, event management, and scenarios where tasks need to be processed by priority.

Max-Heaps and Min-Heaps with Real-World Examples

1. Max-Heap

- A max-heap is structured so that the root node always contains the maximum value.
- **Real-World Example**:
  - **Job Scheduling**: In systems where the most important tasks are processed first, a max-

heap can be used to manage tasks, with higher priority tasks stored at the top.

2. **Min-Heap**

   o A min-heap is structured so that the root node always contains the minimum value.

   o **Real-World Example**:

      ▪ **Dijkstra's Algorithm**: Min-heaps are used to find the shortest path in graph algorithms. The heap helps efficiently retrieve the node with the smallest distance.

      ▪ **Event Simulation**: In simulations, a min-heap can be used to process events in chronological order, where the earliest event is processed first.

3. **Comparison of Operations in Heaps**

   o **Insertion**: A new element is added to the next available position in the last level to maintain the complete binary tree property, then "bubbled up" to maintain the heap property.

   o **Deletion (of the Root)**: The root element (minimum for min-heap or maximum for max-heap) is removed, and the last element is moved to the root position, then "bubbled down" to restore the heap property.

Python's heapq Library and Custom Implementations

Python's heapq module provides a simple and efficient way to implement min-heaps. By default, heapq only supports min-heaps, but a max-heap can be simulated by storing values as their negative counterparts.

1. **Using Python's heapq for Min-Heap**

   python
   import heapq

   ```python
   # Creating a min-heap
   min_heap = []
   heapq.heappush(min_heap, 10)
   heapq.heappush(min_heap, 5)
   heapq.heappush(min_heap, 20)
   heapq.heappush(min_heap, 1)

   # Retrieve the smallest element
   print(heapq.heappop(min_heap))  # Outputs: 1
   ```

   Explanation:

   - heapq.heappush(heap, item): Adds item to the heap, maintaining the heap property.
   - heapq.heappop(heap): Removes and returns the smallest element from the heap.

2. **Using heapq to Simulate a Max-Heap**

```python
python
import heapq

# Creating a max-heap by storing negative values
max_heap = []
heapq.heappush(max_heap, -10)
heapq.heappush(max_heap, -5)
heapq.heappush(max_heap, -20)
heapq.heappush(max_heap, -1)

# Retrieve the largest element (by negating)
print(-heapq.heappop(max_heap))  # Outputs: 20
```

Explanation:

- By pushing negative values, we simulate a max-heap, where the smallest negative value is equivalent to the maximum positive value.

3. **Implementing a Custom Min-Heap from Scratch**

A custom implementation of a min-heap can provide deeper insight into how heap operations work.

```python
python
Copy code
class MinHeap:
    def __init__(self):
```

```python
        self.heap = []

    def insert(self, value):
        self.heap.append(value)
        self._bubble_up(len(self.heap) - 1)

    def remove_min(self):
        if len(self.heap) == 0:
            return None
        if len(self.heap) == 1:
            return self.heap.pop()
        min_value = self.heap[0]
        self.heap[0] = self.heap.pop()
        self._bubble_down(0)
        return min_value

    def _bubble_up(self, index):
        parent_index = (index - 1) // 2
        while index > 0 and self.heap[index] < self.heap[parent_index]:
            self.heap[index], self.heap[parent_index] = self.heap[parent_index], self.heap[index]
            index = parent_index
            parent_index = (index - 1) // 2
```

```python
def _bubble_down(self, index):
    min_index = index
    left_child_index = 2 * index + 1
    right_child_index = 2 * index + 2

    if left_child_index < len(self.heap) and
self.heap[left_child_index] < self.heap[min_index]:
        min_index = left_child_index
    if right_child_index < len(self.heap) and
self.heap[right_child_index] < self.heap[min_index]:
        min_index = right_child_index
    if min_index != index:
        self.heap[index], self.heap[min_index] =
self.heap[min_index], self.heap[index]
        self._bubble_down(min_index)


# Example usage
min_heap = MinHeap()
min_heap.insert(10)
min_heap.insert(5)
min_heap.insert(20)
min_heap.insert(1)
print(min_heap.remove_min())  # Outputs: 1
```

Explanation:

- o **_bubble_up**: After inserting a new element, it's moved upward until the min-heap property is restored.

- o **_bubble_down**: After removing the root, the last element is placed at the root and moved downward until the min-heap property is restored.

4. Implementing a Priority Queue with heapq

Priority queues can be implemented by inserting tuples where the first element is the priority, enabling the heap to prioritize elements.

```python
import heapq

class PriorityQueue:
    def __init__(self):
        self.queue = []

    def enqueue(self, item, priority):
        heapq.heappush(self.queue, (priority, item))

    def dequeue(self):
        if self.queue:
            return heapq.heappop(self.queue)[1]
        return None
```

```
# Example usage
pq = PriorityQueue()
pq.enqueue("task1", 3)
pq.enqueue("task2", 1)  # Higher priority
pq.enqueue("task3", 2)
print(pq.dequeue())  # Outputs: "task2"
```

Explanation:

- o Priority queues are created by storing tuples, where the priority comes first. Lower priority values are dequeued first, making this a min-priority queue.

Real-World Applications of Heaps and Priority Queues

1. **Task Scheduling**
   - o Heaps and priority queues are frequently used in task scheduling systems, where tasks with higher priority (or shorter deadlines) need to be processed first.

2. **Shortest Path Algorithms (Dijkstra's Algorithm)**
   - o Dijkstra's algorithm uses a min-heap to find the shortest path in weighted graphs. By always processing the node with the smallest distance, the algorithm ensures optimal path selection.

3. **Event Simulation Systems**

- o In event-driven simulations, priority queues manage events based on timestamps. The earliest events are processed first, allowing the simulation to proceed chronologically.

4. **Merging Sorted Data**

- o Min-heaps are used to merge sorted arrays efficiently by maintaining a min-heap of the smallest elements across arrays, repeatedly extracting the minimum.

In this chapter, we explored heaps and priority queues, learning how heaps maintain a structure where the minimum or maximum element is always at the root, enabling efficient retrieval and processing. We implemented min-heaps, max-heaps, and priority queues using Python's heapq library and custom classes, and discussed real-world applications such as task scheduling and shortest path algorithms.

In the next chapter, we'll dive into **graph basics** and graph representations, covering fundamental graph terminology, types, and how to implement graphs in Python.

CHAPTER 12: GRAPHS - BASICS AND REPRESENTATIONS

Graphs are a versatile data structure that models relationships between pairs of objects. This chapter covers essential graph terminology, explains different ways to represent graphs in Python (using adjacency lists and matrices), and explores real-world applications such as social networks.

Graph Terminology

1. **What is a Graph?**
   - A graph is a collection of **nodes** (or **vertices**) connected by **edges**.
   - Each edge represents a relationship or connection between two nodes.

2. **Key Terminology**
   - **Nodes (Vertices)**: The elements in a graph, representing entities like users, cities, or devices.
   - **Edges**: The connections between nodes, representing relationships like friendships, roads, or data flows.
   - **Directed Graph (Digraph)**: A graph where each edge has a direction, pointing from one node to

another. Edges in directed graphs are often represented by arrows (e.g., Twitter follows).

o **Undirected Graph**: A graph where edges have no direction, meaning relationships are bidirectional (e.g., Facebook friendships).

o **Weighted Graph**: A graph where edges have weights (or costs), representing distances, costs, or other metrics.

o **Unweighted Graph**: A graph where edges are all treated equally, without associated weights.

o **Path**: A sequence of nodes connected by edges. A path may be simple (no repeated nodes) or a cycle (starts and ends at the same node).

o **Connected Graph**: A graph where there is a path between every pair of nodes.

o **Degree**: The number of edges connected to a node. In directed graphs:

  ▪ **In-degree**: Number of incoming edges to a node.

  ▪ **Out-degree**: Number of outgoing edges from a node.

Representing Graphs in Python

Graphs can be represented in different ways, depending on the use case. The two primary representations are adjacency lists and adjacency matrices.

1. **Adjacency List**

    o An adjacency list represents a graph as a dictionary where each node is a key, and the value is a list of adjacent nodes (nodes directly connected by an edge).

    o Adjacency lists are efficient for storing sparse graphs (graphs with relatively few edges).

Example of an Undirected Graph with an Adjacency List:

python

```python
graph = {
    'A': ['B', 'C'],
    'B': ['A', 'D', 'E'],
    'C': ['A', 'F'],
    'D': ['B'],
    'E': ['B', 'F'],
    'F': ['C', 'E']
}
```

    o **Directed Graph Representation**:

        ▪ Each directed edge is represented by listing only the outgoing nodes for each node.

    o **Weighted Graph Representation**:

- Store tuples of adjacent nodes and weights in the adjacency list.

Example of a Directed Weighted Graph:

python

```
graph = {
    'A': [('B', 3), ('C', 1)],
    'B': [('D', 2)],
    'C': [('F', 4)],
    'D': [],
    'E': [('F', 5)],
    'F': []
}
```

2. **Adjacency Matrix**
   - An adjacency matrix represents a graph as a 2D array (matrix), where the element at row i and column j indicates whether there is an edge from node i to node j.
   - This approach is efficient for dense graphs (graphs with many edges), but for large sparse graphs, it can be memory-intensive.
   - In an unweighted graph, a 1 represents an edge and 0 represents no edge. In a weighted graph, the matrix can store the weight instead of 1.

Example of an Adjacency Matrix for an Unweighted Undirected Graph:

- Nodes: A, B, C, D

python

```
# A  B  C  D
# Matrix for: A -- B, A -- C, B -- D
adj_matrix = [
  [0, 1, 1, 0],  # A
  [1, 0, 0, 1],  # B
  [1, 0, 0, 0],  # C
  [0, 1, 0, 0]   # D
]
```

- **Weighted Graph Matrix**:
  - Instead of 1 and 0, use the weights directly in the matrix to represent weighted edges.

Example of an Adjacency Matrix for a Weighted Directed Graph:

- Nodes: A, B, C

python

```
# A -> B (weight 3), A -> C (weight 1), B -> C (weight 4)
adj_matrix = [
```

```
    [0, 3, 1],  # A
    [0, 0, 4],  # B
    [0, 0, 0]   # C
]
```

3. Python Code for Building a Graph with Adjacency Lists

```python
class Graph:
    def __init__(self):
        self.graph = {}

    def add_edge(self, node, neighbor, directed=False, weight=None):
        if node not in self.graph:
            self.graph[node] = []
        if weight is None:
            self.graph[node].append(neighbor)
        else:
            self.graph[node].append((neighbor, weight))
        if not directed:
            if neighbor not in self.graph:
                self.graph[neighbor] = []
            if weight is None:
                self.graph[neighbor].append(node)
```

```python
        else:
            self.graph[neighbor].append((node, weight))

    def display(self):
        for node, neighbors in self.graph.items():
            print(f"{node} -> {neighbors}")

# Example usage
g = Graph()
g.add_edge("A", "B")
g.add_edge("A", "C")
g.add_edge("B", "D", directed=True, weight=2)
g.display()
```

Real-World Examples of Graphs

1. **Social Networks**
   - Graphs are commonly used in social networks to represent relationships between users.
     - **Nodes**: Users
     - **Edges**: Friendships (undirected) or follows (directed)
   - For instance, Facebook friendships form an undirected graph, whereas Twitter's follow relationships form a directed graph.
2. **Web Page Links**

o The web itself is a large directed graph, where each webpage is a node, and hyperlinks are directed edges connecting pages.

o Search engines use this graph structure to rank and retrieve relevant pages through algorithms like PageRank.

3. **Transportation Networks**

o Cities, airports, or train stations can be represented as nodes, and routes between them as edges. In such graphs:

- **Nodes**: Cities or stations
- **Edges**: Routes between them, potentially weighted by distance or time.

o This graph structure is useful in shortest path algorithms (like Dijkstra's) for finding optimal travel routes.

4. **Dependency Graphs**

o Graphs are used to represent dependencies between tasks or components, often in project management or software compilation.

o **Nodes**: Tasks or modules

o **Edges**: Dependencies between tasks (e.g., Task A must complete before Task B can start).

o Directed Acyclic Graphs (DAGs) are often used to model such dependencies, as they prevent cycles.

5. Electric Circuits

- o Electric circuits can be modeled as graphs where nodes represent components like resistors or capacitors, and edges represent connections (wires) between them.

- o This representation helps in analyzing circuit properties such as paths and loops, which are crucial in understanding circuit behavior.

In this chapter, we explored the basics of graphs, covering fundamental terminology like nodes, edges, directed/undirected graphs, and weighted graphs. We discussed two primary representations—adjacency lists and adjacency matrices—and implemented both in Python. We also examined real-world applications, including social networks, web page links, and transportation networks, where graphs are commonly used.

In the next chapter, we'll delve into **graph traversal algorithms**, including Depth-First Search (DFS) and Breadth-First Search (BFS), and explore how they are used to solve practical problems in graph theory.

CHAPTER 13: GRAPH TRAVERSAL - DFS AND BFS

Graph traversal is essential for exploring and analyzing graphs. This chapter covers two foundational traversal algorithms: Depth-First Search (DFS) and Breadth-First Search (BFS). We'll implement both in Python and explore real-world applications, such as pathfinding in navigation systems.

Depth-First Search (DFS) and Breadth-First Search (BFS)

1. **Depth-First Search (DFS)**

   o DFS explores as far down each branch as possible before backtracking. It prioritizes visiting deeper nodes before moving horizontally to other nodes at the same depth level.

   o DFS can be implemented using recursion (which implicitly uses a call stack) or iteratively using an explicit stack data structure.

   o **DFS Properties**:

- Can be used to explore all nodes connected to a starting node.
- Useful for detecting cycles, finding connected components, and solving problems where exploring all possible paths is required.

2. **Breadth-First Search (BFS)**

   o BFS explores all neighbors of a node before moving to the next level. It prioritizes visiting nodes in layers, making it ideal for finding the shortest path in an unweighted graph.

   o BFS is implemented using a queue, where nodes are visited level by level.

   o **BFS Properties**:

     - Guarantees the shortest path in terms of the number of edges in unweighted graphs.
     - Useful in shortest path algorithms and finding the shortest distance between nodes.

Implementing DFS and BFS in Python

1. **Depth-First Search (DFS) Implementation**

   Recursive DFS:

o Recursive DFS is implemented by calling the function recursively on each unvisited neighbor until all nodes have been visited.

python

```python
def dfs_recursive(graph, node, visited=None):
    if visited is None:
        visited = set()
    visited.add(node)
    print(node, end=" ")
    for neighbor in graph[node]:
        if neighbor not in visited:
            dfs_recursive(graph, neighbor, visited)
    return visited


# Example usage
graph = {
    'A': ['B', 'C'],
    'B': ['A', 'D', 'E'],
    'C': ['A', 'F'],
    'D': ['B'],
    'E': ['B', 'F'],
    'F': ['C', 'E']
}
print("DFS Recursive:", end=" ")
dfs_recursive(graph, 'A')  # Outputs: A B D E F C
```

Iterative DFS:

o Iterative DFS can be implemented using a stack. Nodes are added to the stack and processed one by one, with their unvisited neighbors pushed onto the stack.

```python
def dfs_iterative(graph, start):
    visited = set()
    stack = [start]
    while stack:
        node = stack.pop()
        if node not in visited:
            print(node, end=" ")
            visited.add(node)
            # Add neighbors in reverse order for consistent traversal
            for neighbor in reversed(graph[node]):
                if neighbor not in visited:
                    stack.append(neighbor)
    return visited


print("\nDFS Iterative:", end=" ")
dfs_iterative(graph, 'A')  # Outputs: A C F E B D
```

2. Breadth-First Search (BFS) Implementation

BFS is implemented using a queue, where nodes are processed level by level. Each node's neighbors are added to the queue in the order they are discovered, allowing nodes to be processed in a breadthwise fashion.

```python
from collections import deque

def bfs(graph, start):
    visited = set()
    queue = deque([start])
    visited.add(start)
    while queue:
        node = queue.popleft()
        print(node, end=" ")
        for neighbor in graph[node]:
            if neighbor not in visited:
                visited.add(neighbor)
                queue.append(neighbor)
    return visited

print("\nBFS:", end=" ")
bfs(graph, 'A')  # Outputs: A B C D E F
```

Real-World Applications of DFS and BFS

1. **Pathfinding in Navigation Systems**
   - o BFS is commonly used in navigation systems and maps for finding the shortest path in terms of distance or hops (edges) between two locations, especially in unweighted graphs where each edge has equal weight.
   - o DFS can be used to explore all possible paths, which is helpful in finding alternate routes or paths that visit every location exactly once.

2. **Web Crawling**
   - o Web crawlers use graph traversal algorithms to explore the internet. Each webpage is a node, and links between pages are edges.
   - o **BFS** is often used to prioritize exploring "closer" pages to the current one, while **DFS** can be used to fully explore a website before moving to unrelated sites.

3. **Detecting Cycles in Graphs**
   - o DFS is effective for detecting cycles in graphs, especially directed graphs. If DFS encounters a previously visited node that's not the direct parent, a cycle exists.
   - o This application is particularly useful in detecting circular dependencies in systems like package managers or build systems.

4. **Finding Connected Components**

   o DFS and BFS can be used to identify all connected components in an undirected graph. A connected component is a subset of nodes such that each node is reachable from any other node within the component.

   o This is useful in social networks to identify groups or clusters of connected users.

5. **Solving Puzzles and Mazes**

   o Both DFS and BFS can be used to solve maze problems. **DFS** is useful for exploring all possible paths, while **BFS** is preferred for finding the shortest path from the start to the goal in an unweighted maze.

6. **Topological Sorting (Using DFS)**

   o In directed acyclic graphs (DAGs), DFS can be used for topological sorting, which is a linear ordering of nodes such that each directed edge points from earlier to later in the ordering.

   o This is useful in project scheduling, where tasks depend on the completion of other tasks.

In this chapter, we explored graph traversal algorithms, focusing on Depth-First Search (DFS) and Breadth-First Search (BFS). We implemented both traversal methods in Python and discussed their applications, such as pathfinding in navigation systems, web crawling, cycle detection, and solving mazes. Understanding these traversal techniques is foundational for working with graphs and is essential for solving complex graph-related problems.

In the next chapter, we'll dive into **shortest path algorithms**, exploring algorithms like Dijkstra's and Bellman-Ford, which are essential for efficient pathfinding in weighted graphs.

CHAPTER 14: SHORTEST PATH ALGORITHMS

Shortest path algorithms are essential for solving problems in routing, logistics, and network optimization. In this chapter, we'll cover two primary algorithms for finding the shortest path in graphs: **Dijkstra's** and **Bellman-Ford**. We'll discuss their applications in routing and logistics and provide Python implementations with example cases.

Dijkstra's and Bellman-Ford Algorithms

1. **Dijkstra's Algorithm**
   o **Purpose**: Dijkstra's algorithm finds the shortest path from a starting node to all other nodes in a graph with non-negative edge weights.
   o **Process**:
     ▪ It starts from the source node, updating the shortest known distance to each reachable node.

- Nodes are processed based on the minimum distance from the source, often using a priority queue to efficiently retrieve the closest node.
- Once a node has been visited, its shortest path is known and does not need to be updated.

o **Time Complexity**: $O((V + E) \log V)$, where V is the number of vertices, and E is the number of edges.

o **Limitations**: Dijkstra's algorithm cannot handle graphs with negative edge weights, as it assumes that adding edges can only increase the distance.

2. **Bellman-Ford Algorithm**

o **Purpose**: The Bellman-Ford algorithm finds the shortest path from a source node to all other nodes in a graph, including graphs with negative edge weights.

o **Process**:

- It iterates through each edge and relaxes it, updating the shortest path to each node as it finds smaller distances.
- This process is repeated up to $V - 1$ times, where V is the number of vertices.

- If there is a shorter path after V - 1 iterations, the graph contains a negative-weight cycle.

  o **Time Complexity**: O(V * E), making it slower than Dijkstra's on large graphs but suitable for graphs with negative weights.

  o **Limitations**: The Bellman-Ford algorithm is slower for dense graphs and not optimal for large networks with positive weights.

Applications in Routing and Logistics

1. **Navigation Systems and GPS**

   o Dijkstra's algorithm is commonly used in GPS navigation systems to find the shortest driving route, where distances between locations are represented as edge weights.

   o Bellman-Ford can be used in networks where the edges might have negative values, such as representing tolls, traffic delays, or other variable costs.

2. **Network Routing Protocols**

   o Both algorithms are used in network routing to determine the shortest and most efficient paths for data packets to travel across a network.

- o Dijkstra's algorithm is the basis for the Open Shortest Path First (OSPF) protocol, widely used in IP routing.

3. **Supply Chain and Logistics Optimization**
   - o Shortest path algorithms help optimize logistics, such as finding the shortest or least costly path between distribution centers and stores.
   - o They are also used in vehicle routing problems to determine the most efficient routes for deliveries, minimizing fuel costs and travel time.

4. **Financial Arbitrage Detection**
   - o Bellman-Ford can detect negative cycles in graphs, which represent potential arbitrage opportunities in currency exchange graphs where nodes are currencies and edges are exchange rates.

Python Implementations with Example Cases

1. **Dijkstra's Algorithm Implementation**

   Python Code for Dijkstra's Algorithm Using heapq:

   - o We use a priority queue (min-heap) to keep track of nodes with the smallest known distance from the source.

   python

```python
import heapq

def dijkstra(graph, start):
    # Initialize distances and priority queue
    distances = {node: float('inf') for node in graph}
    distances[start] = 0
    priority_queue = [(0, start)]  # (distance, node)

    while priority_queue:
        current_distance, current_node = heapq.heappop(priority_queue)

        # Skip if we already found a shorter path
        if current_distance > distances[current_node]:
            continue

        # Update distances to neighbors
        for neighbor, weight in graph[current_node]:
            distance = current_distance + weight
            if distance < distances[neighbor]:
                distances[neighbor] = distance
                heapq.heappush(priority_queue, (distance, neighbor))

    return distances
```

```
# Example graph
graph = {
    'A': [('B', 1), ('C', 4)],
    'B': [('A', 1), ('C', 2), ('D', 5)],
    'C': [('A', 4), ('B', 2), ('D', 1)],
    'D': [('B', 5), ('C', 1)]
}


# Run Dijkstra's algorithm
print(dijkstra(graph, 'A'))  # Outputs shortest distances from
A
```

Explanation:

- o Each node's initial distance is set to infinity, except the start node, which has a distance of zero.
- o For each node, we update the shortest known distance to its neighbors if a shorter path is found.
- o Once a node is visited (removed from the priority queue), it's processed and won't be revisited.

2. **Bellman-Ford Algorithm Implementation**

Python Code for Bellman-Ford Algorithm:

o The Bellman-Ford algorithm iterates over all edges to relax them up to V - 1 times, where V is the number of nodes.

```python
def bellman_ford(graph, start):
    # Initialize distances
    distances = {node: float('inf') for node in graph}
    distances[start] = 0

    # Relax edges up to V-1 times
    for _ in range(len(graph) - 1):
        for node in graph:
            for neighbor, weight in graph[node]:
                if distances[node] + weight < distances[neighbor]:
                    distances[neighbor] = distances[node] + weight

    # Check for negative-weight cycles
    for node in graph:
        for neighbor, weight in graph[node]:
            if distances[node] + weight < distances[neighbor]:
                raise ValueError("Graph contains a negative-weight cycle")
```

return distances

# Example graph with negative weights
graph = {
    'A': [('B', 1), ('C', 4)],
    'B': [('C', -2), ('D', 2)],
    'C': [('D', 1)],
    'D': []
}

Run Bellman-Ford algorithm
print(bellman_ford(graph, 'A'))   # Outputs shortest distances from A

Explanation:

- Each node's initial distance is set to infinity, except for the start node, which is set to zero.
- For V - 1 iterations, each edge is relaxed. If a shorter path to a neighboring node is found, it's updated.
- After V - 1 relaxations, if we find a shorter path, there is a negative-weight cycle in the graph.

3. **Example Application: Shortest Path in a Logistics Network**

Suppose we have a network of warehouses and need to find the shortest route from one warehouse to all others.

```python
# Warehouse network with distances
warehouse_graph = {
    'Warehouse A': [('Warehouse B', 10), ('Warehouse C', 20)],
    'Warehouse B': [('Warehouse C', 5), ('Warehouse D', 15)],
    'Warehouse C': [('Warehouse D', 10)],
    'Warehouse D': []
}

# Use Dijkstra's algorithm to find shortest paths from Warehouse A
shortest_paths = dijkstra(warehouse_graph, 'Warehouse A')
print("Shortest paths from Warehouse A:", shortest_paths)
```

Explanation:

o This example demonstrates finding the shortest route from a starting warehouse to all other warehouses.

o Using Dijkstra's algorithm, we efficiently calculate the shortest path based on the distance between warehouses, helping in logistics planning.

In this chapter, we explored two key shortest path algorithms: **Dijkstra's** and **Bellman-Ford**. Dijkstra's algorithm is highly efficient for graphs with non-negative weights, while Bellman-Ford is versatile, handling graphs with negative weights and detecting negative cycles. We implemented both algorithms in Python and examined applications in real-world scenarios, including navigation, network routing, logistics, and finance.

In the next chapter, we'll dive into **sorting algorithms**, covering essential techniques like merge sort and quicksort, and discussing when and how to use them effectively.

CHAPTER 15: SORTING ALGORITHMS - BASICS

Sorting is a fundamental operation in computer science, critical for organizing and optimizing data for quick access and retrieval. This chapter introduces the importance of sorting, provides an overview of basic sorting algorithms (bubble sort, selection sort, and insertion sort), and includes Python implementations with guidance on when to use each.

Introduction to Sorting

1. **Why Sorting is Essential**
   - **Improves Efficiency**: Sorting data enables efficient searching, filtering, and organization, making operations like binary search possible (which requires sorted data).
   - **Data Organization**: Sorted data is easier to understand, manage, and present, essential for applications such as databases, spreadsheets, and reports.
   - **Algorithm Optimization**: Many algorithms assume sorted data for optimal performance, such as search algorithms and certain optimization algorithms.

2. **Types of Sorting Algorithms**
   - Sorting algorithms can generally be categorized by their complexity, approach (comparison-based or non-comparison-based), and use cases.
   - In this chapter, we focus on **comparison-based** algorithms, which rely on comparing elements to determine order.

Overview of Common Algorithms

1. **Bubble Sort**

   o **Description**: Bubble sort repeatedly steps through the list, comparing adjacent elements and swapping them if they're in the wrong order. The largest unsorted elements "bubble" up to the correct position in each pass.

   o **Time Complexity**: $O(n^2)$ in the average and worst case.

   o **When to Use**: Bubble sort is simple but inefficient for large lists. It is best used for educational purposes or when sorting very small datasets.

Python Code for Bubble Sort:

python
```python
def bubble_sort(arr):
    n = len(arr)
    for i in range(n):
        for j in range(0, n - i - 1):
            if arr[j] > arr[j + 1]:
                arr[j], arr[j + 1] = arr[j + 1], arr[j]
    return arr


# Example usage
arr = [64, 34, 25, 12, 22, 11, 90]
```

```python
print("Sorted array:", bubble_sort(arr))   # Outputs sorted
array
```

2. **Selection Sort**

   o **Description**: Selection sort divides the list into sorted and unsorted portions. It finds the minimum (or maximum) element in the unsorted portion and swaps it with the first unsorted element, expanding the sorted portion by one.

   o **Time Complexity**: $O(n^2)$ in all cases, as it always iterates through the unsorted portion to find the minimum.

   o **When to Use**: Selection sort is more efficient than bubble sort for minimizing the number of swaps, but it's still inefficient for large datasets.

Python Code for Selection Sort:

```python
python
def selection_sort(arr):
    n = len(arr)
    for i in range(n):
        min_idx = i
        for j in range(i + 1, n):
            if arr[j] < arr[min_idx]:
                min_idx = j
```

```
        arr[i], arr[min_idx] = arr[min_idx], arr[i]
    return arr
```

```
# Example usage
arr = [64, 25, 12, 22, 11]
print("Sorted array:", selection_sort(arr))  # Outputs sorted array
```

3. **Insertion Sort**

   o **Description**: Insertion sort builds the sorted portion of the list one element at a time by repeatedly inserting each unsorted element into its correct position in the sorted portion.

   o **Time Complexity**: $O(n^2)$ in the average and worst case, but $O(n)$ for nearly sorted lists.

   o **When to Use**: Insertion sort is efficient for small datasets or lists that are already mostly sorted. It's also suitable for data structures that allow efficient insertions, such as linked lists.

Python Code for Insertion Sort:

```python
def insertion_sort(arr):
    for i in range(1, len(arr)):
        key = arr[i]
```

```
    j = i - 1
    while j >= 0 and arr[j] > key:
        arr[j + 1] = arr[j]
        j -= 1
    arr[j + 1] = key
return arr


# Example usage
arr = [12, 11, 13, 5, 6]
print("Sorted array:", insertion_sort(arr))  # Outputs sorted
array
```

When to Use Each Algorithm

- **Bubble Sort**:
  - Use for very small datasets where simplicity is preferred, or for educational purposes to understand sorting concepts.
  - Inefficient for larger datasets due to its high number of comparisons and swaps.
- **Selection Sort**:
  - Suitable when memory writes are expensive and need to be minimized, as it performs fewer swaps than bubble sort.
  - Not ideal for large datasets due to its $O(n^2)$ complexity.

- **Insertion Sort**:
  - Best for small or nearly sorted datasets, where it can perform well due to fewer shifts.
  - Useful for sorting data incrementally as new items are added, particularly in cases like maintaining a sorted list with frequent inserts.

Real-World Example: Sorting a List of Students by Grades

Imagine a scenario where you have a small list of students with their grades, and you want to sort them in ascending order of grades.

python

```python
students = [
    {"name": "Alice", "grade": 88},
    {"name": "Bob", "grade": 72},
    {"name": "Charlie", "grade": 91},
    {"name": "Diana", "grade": 84}
]


def sort_students_by_grade(students):
    for i in range(1, len(students)):
        key = students[i]
        j = i - 1
        while j >= 0 and students[j]["grade"] > key["grade"]:
            students[j + 1] = students[j]
```

```
        j -= 1
     students[j + 1] = key
  return students
```

```
sorted_students = sort_students_by_grade(students)
for student in sorted_students:
  print(f"{student['name']} - Grade: {student['grade']}")
```

Explanation:

- This uses **insertion sort** to efficiently sort the small list of students by grade.
- The result is a sorted list that displays each student's name and grade in ascending order.

In this chapter, we explored three fundamental sorting algorithms: **bubble sort**, **selection sort**, and **insertion sort**. We implemented each algorithm in Python, discussed their time complexities, and outlined when to use each one. While these algorithms are primarily educational, they offer insight into sorting techniques and are useful for small or nearly sorted datasets.

In the next chapter, we'll explore **efficient sorting algorithms**, focusing on merge sort and quicksort, which are more suitable for large datasets.

CHAPTER 16: EFFICIENT SORTING - MERGE SORT AND QUICK SORT

When sorting large datasets, efficient algorithms like merge sort and quicksort are essential due to their faster average and worst-case performance compared to basic sorting algorithms. This chapter provides a step-by-step explanation of merge sort and quicksort, explores their real-world relevance, and includes Python implementations.

Merge Sort and Quick Sort Explained with Step-by-Step Examples

1. **Merge Sort**
   - **Description**: Merge sort is a divide-and-conquer algorithm that divides the list into two halves, recursively sorts each half, and then merges the sorted halves.
   - **Process**:
     1. **Divide** the list into two halves until each sublist has only one element (base case).
     2. **Merge** the sorted sublists by comparing elements and placing them in the correct order.
   - **Time Complexity**: O(n log n) in all cases, making it efficient for large datasets.
   - **Space Complexity**: O(n), as it requires additional memory for merging.

   Step-by-Step Example:

   - Given list: [38, 27, 43, 3, 9, 82, 10]
   - Step 1: Divide until each sublist has one element:

- [38, 27, 43, 3] and [9, 82, 10]
- [38, 27], [43, 3], [9, 82], [10]
- [38], [27], [43], [3], [9], [82], [10]

  o Step 2: Merge:
  - [27, 38], [3, 43], [9, 10, 82]
  - [3, 27, 38, 43] and [9, 10, 82]
  - Final merged list: [3, 9, 10, 27, 38, 43, 82]

Python Code for Merge Sort:

```python
def merge_sort(arr):
    if len(arr) <= 1:
        return arr

    # Divide
    mid = len(arr) // 2
    left_half = merge_sort(arr[:mid])
    right_half = merge_sort(arr[mid:])

    # Merge
    return merge(left_half, right_half)

def merge(left, right):
    result = []
    i = j = 0
```

```python
        # Merge while both lists have elements
        while i < len(left) and j < len(right):
            if left[i] < right[j]:
                result.append(left[i])
                i += 1
            else:
                result.append(right[j])
                j += 1

        # Append any remaining elements
        result.extend(left[i:])
        result.extend(right[j:])
        return result

    # Example usage
    arr = [38, 27, 43, 3, 9, 82, 10]
    print("Sorted array:", merge_sort(arr))  # Outputs: [3, 9, 10,
    27, 38, 43, 82]
```

2. **Quick Sort**

   o **Description**: Quick sort is a divide-and-conquer algorithm that partitions the list into elements less than and greater than a chosen **pivot** element, then recursively sorts each partition.

   o **Process**:

1. Choose a pivot element (usually the first, last, or middle element).
2. **Partition** the list, placing all elements smaller than the pivot on the left and larger ones on the right.
3. Recursively apply quicksort on the left and right partitions.

o **Time Complexity**: Average O(n log n), but worst-case O(n^2) if the pivot consistently divides the list unevenly (often mitigated by using random pivots).

o **Space Complexity**: O(log n) for recursive calls, making it more memory-efficient than merge sort.

Step-by-Step Example:

o Given list: [38, 27, 43, 3, 9, 82, 10]
o Step 1: Choose a pivot (e.g., 10).
o Step 2: Partition:

   ▪ Left of 10: [3, 9]
   ▪ Pivot 10
   ▪ Right of 10: [38, 27, 43, 82]

o Step 3: Recursively apply quicksort:
   ▪ [3, 9] remains [3, 9]
   ▪ [38, 27, 43, 82] -> after partitioning around 43: [27, 38] and [82]

o   Final sorted list: [3, 9, 10, 27, 38, 43, 82]

Python Code for Quick Sort:

```python
python
def quick_sort(arr):
  if len(arr) <= 1:
    return arr

  pivot = arr[len(arr) // 2]  # Choose the middle element as the pivot
  left = [x for x in arr if x < pivot]
  middle = [x for x in arr if x == pivot]
  right = [x for x in arr if x > pivot]

  return quick_sort(left) + middle + quick_sort(right)

# Example usage
arr = [38, 27, 43, 3, 9, 82, 10]
print("Sorted array:", quick_sort(arr))  # Outputs: [3, 9, 10, 27, 38, 43, 82]
```

Real-World Relevance of Merge Sort and Quick Sort

1. **Large Data Sorting in Databases and Data Processing**
   o   **Merge Sort**: Since merge sort divides data into smaller chunks, it can be implemented to handle

massive datasets by dividing them into manageable parts, sorting them, and then merging them. This is commonly used in **external sorting**, where data too large to fit in memory is sorted by dividing it into smaller, sorted segments.

- **Quick Sort**: Used in many internal sorting algorithms due to its high efficiency for in-memory sorting. Quick sort's ability to sort in-place and use a small memory footprint makes it popular in database management systems and libraries like Python's own sorting functions.

2. **System and File Management**

- Sorting is essential in operating systems, especially in managing files or processes. File systems that sort file names or manage search results often use quicksort, as it efficiently handles large numbers of entries.

3. **Scientific and Financial Data Analysis**

- Quick sort and merge sort are both used to efficiently organize large data collections for further analysis. For example, sorting financial transactions or experimental data by value enables quick access to specific data points and helps with statistics and data visualization.

When to Use Merge Sort vs. Quick Sort

- **Merge Sort**:
  - Best for very large datasets, especially when data cannot fit in memory (external sorting).
  - Preferred when a stable sort is required (i.e., the relative order of equal elements is maintained).
  - Often used in linked list sorting, as merge sort does not require random access to elements.

- **Quick Sort**:
  - Often faster for in-memory sorting due to lower constant factors in its complexity.
  - Suitable for applications where in-place sorting is necessary, as it doesn't require additional storage.
  - Popular in practical applications like database sorting and language libraries (e.g., Python's sort()).

In this chapter, we explored two efficient sorting algorithms: **merge sort** and **quick sort**. Merge sort's O(n log n) complexity and stable sorting make it ideal for large, external datasets, while quicksort's efficiency and in-place sorting capability make it popular for internal, memory-efficient sorting. We implemented both algorithms in Python and discussed their applications in large data sorting, file management, and data analysis.

In the next chapter, we'll move on to **search algorithms** and cover linear and binary search, examining their efficiencies, use cases, and Python implementations.

CHAPTER 17: SEARCH ALGORITHMS - LINEAR AND BINARY SEARCH

Searching is a core operation in data processing, enabling us to retrieve specific elements from a collection. This chapter covers two foundational search algorithms, **linear search** and **binary**

search, explaining their differences, implementing them in Python, and discussing real-world applications.

Linear Search and Binary Search Explained

1. **Linear Search**
   - **Description**: Linear search is a straightforward search algorithm that scans each element in a list sequentially until it finds the target element or reaches the end of the list.
   - **Process**:
     - Start from the first element and compare each element with the target.
     - If a match is found, return the index of the element.
     - If no match is found after reaching the end, return a failure indicator (e.g., -1 or None).
   - **Time Complexity**: O(n) in both the average and worst cases, as each element might need to be checked.
   - **Use Cases**: Useful when dealing with small or unsorted datasets.

2. **Binary Search**
   - **Description**: Binary search is a more efficient algorithm that works on **sorted** lists. It repeatedly

divides the search interval in half, eliminating half of the remaining elements in each step.

- o **Process**:
  - Start with the middle element of the list.
  - If the middle element is equal to the target, return its index.
  - If the target is smaller than the middle element, repeat the search on the left half of the list.
  - If the target is larger, search the right half.
  - Continue until the target is found or the search interval becomes empty.
- o **Time Complexity**: O(log n), making it highly efficient for large, sorted datasets.
- o **Use Cases**: Ideal for applications with sorted data, where high-speed searches are needed.

Implementing Searches in Python

1. **Linear Search Implementation**

Python Code for Linear Search:

```python
def linear_search(arr, target):
    for index, element in enumerate(arr):
        if element == target:
```

```
        return index   # Return the index of the found
element
    return -1  # Target not found
```

```
# Example usage
arr = [10, 23, 45, 70, 11, 15]
print("Index of 70:", linear_search(arr, 70))   # Outputs:
Index of 70: 3
print("Index of 99:", linear_search(arr, 99))   # Outputs:
Index of 99: -1
```

Explanation:

- o Each element is checked in sequence.
- o The function returns the index if the target is found, or -1 if it is not in the list.

2. **Binary Search Implementation**

Python Code for Binary Search (Iterative):

```python
python
def binary_search(arr, target):
    left, right = 0, len(arr) - 1
    while left <= right:
        mid = (left + right) // 2
        if arr[mid] == target:
            return mid
```

```python
    elif arr[mid] < target:
        left = mid + 1
    else:
        right = mid - 1
  return -1  # Target not found
```

```python
# Example usage (list must be sorted)
arr = [11, 15, 23, 45, 70, 88]
print("Index of 70:", binary_search(arr, 70))  # Outputs: Index of 70: 4
print("Index of 99:", binary_search(arr, 99))  # Outputs: Index of 99: -1
```

Python Code for Binary Search (Recursive):

```python
python
def binary_search_recursive(arr, target, left=0, right=None):
    if right is None:
        right = len(arr) - 1

    if left > right:
        return -1  # Target not found

    mid = (left + right) // 2
    if arr[mid] == target:
        return mid
```

```
    elif arr[mid] < target:
        return binary_search_recursive(arr, target, mid + 1,
right)
    else:
        return binary_search_recursive(arr, target, left, mid -
1)


# Example usage
arr = [11, 15, 23, 45, 70, 88]
print("Index of 70:", binary_search_recursive(arr, 70))  #
Outputs: Index of 70: 4
print("Index of 99:", binary_search_recursive(arr, 99))  #
Outputs: Index of 99: -1
```

Explanation:

- o **Iterative Binary Search**: Uses a while loop to adjust the search boundaries based on the target's position relative to the middle element.

- o **Recursive Binary Search**: Calls itself on either the left or right half, adjusting the boundaries with each recursive call.

- o Both implementations assume a sorted list. If the list is not sorted, binary search cannot guarantee correct results.

Real-World Applications in Database and Document Search Systems

1. **Database Indexing**

   o **Binary Search**: Databases often use binary search as part of index structures to quickly locate records within sorted indices. A binary search on an indexed field provides O(log n) access time, greatly speeding up query results.

   o **Linear Search**: In cases where the data is small or not indexed, databases may use linear search, especially when looking through temporary or unsorted results.

2. **Search Engines and Document Search Systems**

   o **Binary Search for Sorted Data**: Inverted indices, which are sorted lists of document IDs associated with keywords, allow search engines to perform binary searches on the index, quickly retrieving relevant documents.

   o **Linear Search for Scanning Documents**: When indexing new documents, linear search is used to process the content of each document sequentially to extract terms and add them to the index.

3. **Product Catalogs and E-commerce Platforms**

   o **Binary Search for Fast Retrieval**: Large online stores maintain sorted catalogs of products by attributes such as price, ratings, or popularity. Binary search enables fast retrieval based on these attributes, allowing users to filter and sort products efficiently.

o **Linear Search for Small or Unsorted Data**: Small datasets, like in niche stores, may use linear search to retrieve information, as the overhead of sorting and indexing may not be necessary.

4. **Spell Checkers and Auto-Complete Systems**

o **Binary Search in Word Lists**: Spell checkers and autocomplete systems use binary search on a sorted dictionary to efficiently find words matching user input.

o **Linear Search in Contextual Scanning**: Linear search is used to scan through recent documents or user history for recently typed terms or context-based suggestions, which may not be sorted.

5. **Data Analytics and Business Intelligence**

o **Binary Search on Sorted Data**: In data analytics, binary search can be used on sorted datasets (e.g., time-series data) to quickly locate specific values or ranges.

o **Linear Search in Exploratory Analysis**: For exploratory data analysis, linear search is often used when filtering data on multiple, unsorted columns where indexing is not yet feasible.

In this chapter, we examined two essential search algorithms: **linear search** and **binary search**. We implemented both in Python, explored their time complexities, and discussed their use cases in real-world applications such as database indexing, search engines, and e-commerce platforms. Linear search is a simple and versatile approach for unsorted data, while binary search offers efficient $O(\log n)$ performance for sorted data, making it ideal for large datasets.

In the next chapter, we'll delve into **recursion and dynamic programming**, introducing recursive problem-solving, memoization, and basic dynamic programming concepts.

CHAPTER 18: RECURSION AND DYNAMIC PROGRAMMING - INTRODUCTION

Recursion and dynamic programming are powerful techniques used to solve complex problems by breaking them down into smaller subproblems. This chapter introduces recursion, explains the basics of dynamic programming, and includes example problems like the Fibonacci sequence.

Introduction to Recursion (Concepts and Pitfalls)

1. **What is Recursion?**
   - Recursion is a technique where a function calls itself in order to solve a problem. Each recursive call tackles a smaller part of the problem, eventually reaching a base case that stops further recursion.
   - **Base Case**: The condition that stops the recursion, preventing an infinite loop.
   - **Recursive Case**: The part of the function that calls itself with modified arguments, moving toward the base case.

2. **Example: Calculating Factorials**
   - A factorial of a number n (denoted n!) is the product of all positive integers from 1 to n.

o **Recursive Definition**: n! = n * (n - 1)! with a base case of 0! = 1.

Python Code for Factorial:

```python
def factorial(n):
    if n == 0:
        return 1  # Base case
    return n * factorial(n - 1)  # Recursive case


# Example usage
print(factorial(5))  # Outputs: 120
```

3. **Common Pitfalls of Recursion**
   o **Missing Base Case**: If the base case is not defined, the recursion will continue indefinitely, leading to a stack overflow.
   o **Excessive Function Calls**: Recursive functions can lead to redundant calculations, especially if they revisit the same subproblems multiple times, causing inefficiency.
   o **Stack Limitations**: Each recursive call adds a new frame to the call stack, which can lead to a stack overflow for large inputs.

Dynamic Programming Basics and Problem-Solving Approach

1. **What is Dynamic Programming (DP)?**

   o Dynamic programming is an optimization technique that solves problems by breaking them down into overlapping subproblems, solving each subproblem once, and storing the results for future reference.

   o DP is commonly used to optimize recursive solutions, especially for problems with overlapping subproblems and optimal substructure (where the optimal solution to a problem depends on the optimal solutions to its subproblems).

2. **Two Key Concepts in Dynamic Programming**

   o **Memoization**: A top-down approach where results of subproblems are stored in a data structure (like a dictionary or array) to avoid redundant calculations.

   o **Tabulation**: A bottom-up approach where the problem is solved by iteratively building up solutions to subproblems and storing them in a table or array.

3. **Problem-Solving Approach with Dynamic Programming**

   o **Step 1**: Define the problem in terms of smaller subproblems.

   o **Step 2**: Identify overlapping subproblems that are solved multiple times.

   o **Step 3**: Choose between memoization or tabulation based on problem requirements.

   o **Step 4**: Implement the solution and use memoization or a table to store results of subproblems.

Example Problems: Fibonacci Sequence

The Fibonacci sequence is a classic example that demonstrates the benefits of dynamic programming over plain recursion.

1. **Recursive Solution (Without Memoization)**

   o **Definition**: $Fib(n) = Fib(n - 1) + Fib(n - 2)$ with base cases $Fib(0) = 0$ and $Fib(1) = 1$.

   o **Problem**: This approach recalculates the same values multiple times, resulting in exponential time complexity, $O(2^n)$.

Python Code for Fibonacci (Plain Recursion):

```python
python
def fibonacci_recursive(n):
    if n <= 1:
        return n  # Base cases
    return fibonacci_recursive(n - 1) + fibonacci_recursive(n - 2)


# Example usage
```

```python
print(fibonacci_recursive(10))  # Outputs: 55
```

2. Optimized Solution Using Memoization

- Memoization reduces the time complexity to O(n) by storing previously calculated Fibonacci values, avoiding redundant calculations.

Python Code for Fibonacci (Recursion with Memoization):

```python
python
def fibonacci_memo(n, memo={}):
    if n in memo:
        return memo[n]  # Return cached result
    if n <= 1:
        return n  # Base cases
    memo[n] = fibonacci_memo(n - 1, memo) + fibonacci_memo(n - 2, memo)
    return memo[n]


# Example usage
print(fibonacci_memo(10))  # Outputs: 55
```

Explanation:

- Each Fibonacci number is calculated only once and stored in memo.

    o   When a previously computed Fibonacci number is needed, it is retrieved from memo instead of recalculated.

3. **Optimized Solution Using Tabulation (Bottom-Up DP)**

    o   Instead of recursion, a bottom-up approach iteratively builds the solution from smaller subproblems.

Python Code for Fibonacci (Tabulation):

python
```
def fibonacci_tabulation(n):
    if n <= 1:
        return n
    fib = [0] * (n + 1)
    fib[1] = 1
    for i in range(2, n + 1):
        fib[i] = fib[i - 1] + fib[i - 2]
    return fib[n]


# Example usage
print(fibonacci_tabulation(10))  # Outputs: 55
```
Explanation:

    o   We initialize an array fib to store Fibonacci numbers.

- o Starting from Fib(2), we fill the array by summing the previous two values, ensuring each Fibonacci number is calculated only once.

4. **Space-Optimized Tabulation for Fibonacci**

- o Since Fibonacci only requires the last two values, we can use variables instead of an array to store intermediate results, reducing space complexity to O(1).

Python Code for Space-Optimized Fibonacci:

```python
def fibonacci_optimized(n):
    if n <= 1:
        return n
    a, b = 0, 1
    for _ in range(2, n + 1):
        a, b = b, a + b
    return b


# Example usage
print(fibonacci_optimized(10))  # Outputs: 55
```

Explanation:

- o We use two variables, a and b, to store the last two Fibonacci numbers, updating them iteratively.

o This approach achieves both O(n) time complexity and O(1) space complexity.

Real-World Applications of Recursion and Dynamic Programming

1. **Pathfinding and Navigation**
   - o Dynamic programming is used in shortest path algorithms like Dijkstra's and Floyd-Warshall to store intermediate path costs, allowing for efficient path calculations in routing systems and GPS.

2. **Data Compression and Pattern Matching**
   - o Algorithms like the Longest Common Subsequence (LCS) and Longest Increasing Subsequence (LIS) use dynamic programming to efficiently match and compress patterns in strings and sequences.

3. **Financial Analysis and Stock Trading**
   - o In stock trading, DP algorithms optimize decisions based on previous outcomes, such as calculating maximum profit by identifying the best days to buy and sell stocks.

4. **Game Development and AI**
   - o Recursive algorithms and dynamic programming are used to implement decision-making in games, where AI must consider multiple possible outcomes

efficiently, such as in minimax algorithms for chess and tic-tac-toe.

5. **Resource Allocation and Scheduling**

   o DP is widely applied in optimizing resource allocation, such as in knapsack and scheduling problems, where tasks must be scheduled or allocated based on certain constraints and goals.

In this chapter, we explored recursion, dynamic programming, and how they relate to each other. We covered key concepts, including base cases and recursive cases in recursion, as well as memoization and tabulation in dynamic programming. Using the Fibonacci sequence, we demonstrated different implementations and optimizations. We also discussed real-world applications where these techniques improve performance in complex problem-solving scenarios.

In the next chapter, we'll explore **advanced dynamic programming**, covering more complex problems like the knapsack problem, longest common subsequence, and matrix chain multiplication, along with their solutions.

CHAPTER 19: DYNAMIC PROGRAMMING TECHNIQUES

Dynamic programming (DP) allows us to solve complex problems efficiently by breaking them down into overlapping subproblems. In this chapter, we'll compare **memoization** and **tabulation**, explore solutions to classic DP problems (like the **knapsack** and **longest common subsequence** problems), and provide practical coding tips for implementing DP.

Memoization vs. Tabulation

1. **Memoization (Top-Down DP)**
   - Memoization involves solving a problem recursively while storing results of subproblems to avoid redundant calculations.

- o Each subproblem is solved only once and stored in a data structure (usually a dictionary or array). If the same subproblem is needed again, the solution is retrieved from memory instead of recalculated.
- o **Pros**: Memoization is often easier to implement, especially for recursive solutions.
- o **Cons**: Memoization relies on recursion, which may lead to stack overflow issues for very deep recursion (e.g., large inputs).

Example Code (Fibonacci):

python
```python
def fibonacci_memo(n, memo={}):
    if n in memo:
        return memo[n]
    if n <= 1:
        return n
    memo[n] = fibonacci_memo(n - 1, memo) + fibonacci_memo(n - 2, memo)
    return memo[n]
```

2. **Tabulation (Bottom-Up DP)**
   - o Tabulation solves the problem iteratively by building a table from the smallest subproblems up to the full solution.

o A table (array) is filled with solutions to subproblems, starting from the simplest subproblems and working up to the target solution.

o **Pros**: Tabulation is typically more memory-efficient and avoids the risk of stack overflow.

o **Cons**: Tabulation can be less intuitive, especially if one is used to thinking in recursive terms.

Example Code (Fibonacci):

python
Copy code
```
def fibonacci_tab(n):
    if n <= 1:
        return n
    fib = [0] * (n + 1)
    fib[1] = 1
    for i in range(2, n + 1):
        fib[i] = fib[i - 1] + fib[i - 2]
    return fib[n]
```

Solving Classic Problems Using Dynamic Programming

1. **Knapsack Problem**

   o **Problem**: Given a list of items, each with a weight and value, and a maximum weight capacity, find the maximum value that can be obtained without exceeding the weight capacity.

- o **Type**: 0/1 Knapsack (an item can either be included or excluded).
- o **Approach**:
  - Define dp[i][w] as the maximum value obtainable with i items and a weight limit w.
  - Either include the item (if it fits) and add its value, or exclude it. Choose the option that gives the maximum value.

Tabulation Code for Knapsack:

python
```python
def knapsack(values, weights, capacity):
    n = len(values)
    dp = [[0] * (capacity + 1) for _ in range(n + 1)]

    for i in range(1, n + 1):
        for w in range(capacity + 1):
            if weights[i - 1] <= w:
                dp[i][w] = max(dp[i - 1][w], values[i - 1] + dp[i - 1][w - weights[i - 1]])
            else:
                dp[i][w] = dp[i - 1][w]
```

```
return dp[n][capacity]
```

```
# Example usage
values = [60, 100, 120]
weights = [10, 20, 30]
capacity = 50
print("Maximum    value:",    knapsack(values,    weights,
capacity))  # Outputs: 220
```

Explanation:

- o   We iterate over each item and each weight capacity, filling the table dp with the maximum obtainable value.
- o   The solution is found in dp[n][capacity], representing the maximum value using all items up to the weight limit.

2. **Longest Common Subsequence (LCS)**

- o   **Problem**: Given two strings, find the length of their longest subsequence that appears in both strings.
- o   **Approach**:
    - ▪   Define dp[i][j] as the length of the LCS of the first i characters of one string and the first j characters of the other.
    - ▪   If the characters match, the LCS increases by 1. If they don't, take the maximum LCS

found by excluding one character from either string.

Tabulation Code for LCS:

```python
def lcs(str1, str2):
    n, m = len(str1), len(str2)
    dp = [[0] * (m + 1) for _ in range(n + 1)]

    for i in range(1, n + 1):
        for j in range(1, m + 1):
            if str1[i - 1] == str2[j - 1]:
                dp[i][j] = dp[i - 1][j - 1] + 1
            else:
                dp[i][j] = max(dp[i - 1][j], dp[i][j - 1])

    return dp[n][m]


# Example usage
str1 = "AGGTAB"
str2 = "GXTXAYB"
print("Length of LCS:", lcs(str1, str2))  # Outputs: 4
```

Explanation:

- o The table dp stores the length of the LCS for each combination of substrings.
- o The final result, dp[n][m], contains the LCS length of the full strings.

3. **Subset Sum Problem**
   - o **Problem**: Given a set of numbers and a target sum, determine if there exists a subset whose elements add up to the target.
   - o **Approach**:
     - Define dp[i][j] as True if there's a subset of the first i elements with sum j, otherwise False.
     - For each number, either include it in the subset (if it does not exceed the current sum) or exclude it.

Tabulation Code for Subset Sum:

python
```python
def subset_sum(nums, target):
    n = len(nums)
    dp = [[False] * (target + 1) for _ in range(n + 1)]
    dp[0][0] = True  # Sum of 0 is possible with an empty subset

    for i in range(1, n + 1):
```

```
        for j in range(target + 1):
            if j < nums[i - 1]:
                dp[i][j] = dp[i - 1][j]
            else:
                dp[i][j] = dp[i - 1][j] or dp[i - 1][j - nums[i - 1]]


    return dp[n][target]


# Example usage
nums = [3, 34, 4, 12, 5, 2]
target = 9
print("Subset with sum exists:", subset_sum(nums, target))
# Outputs: True
```

Explanation:

- The dp table tracks the possible subset sums for each combination of elements.
- The solution is found in dp[n][target], indicating whether a subset with the target sum exists.

Practical Coding Tips for Implementing Dynamic Programming

1. **Identify Overlapping Subproblems**:
   - Recognize repeated calculations by identifying recursive calls that handle the same inputs multiple

times. These are candidates for memoization or tabulation.

2. **Define Clear State Variables**:
   - o Clearly define what each state variable represents, whether it's the number of items processed, remaining capacity, or the current character position.

3. **Choose Memoization for Recursive Problems**:
   - o When a recursive solution is intuitive, start by implementing it with memoization. This helps avoid stack overflow and can simplify recursive problem-solving.

4. **Optimize Space Where Possible**:
   - o In tabulation, minimize space usage by reusing previous states when only a limited set of past values are needed. For example, use a one-dimensional array or a sliding window approach when possible.

5. **Test with Edge Cases**:
   - o Dynamic programming solutions should handle edge cases, such as empty inputs, minimal values, or maximum capacity constraints. Testing with edge cases ensures robustness.

In this chapter, we explored dynamic programming techniques, comparing **memoization** (top-down) and **tabulation** (bottom-up). We solved classic problems like the **knapsack problem, longest**

common subsequence, and **subset sum**, demonstrating different approaches to breaking down complex problems into simpler subproblems. Lastly, we covered practical tips for implementing DP solutions effectively.

In the next chapter, we'll dive deeper into **graph algorithms with dynamic programming**, focusing on advanced techniques for pathfinding, network flows, and cycle detection.

CHAPTER 20: GREEDY ALGORITHMS

Greedy algorithms are a class of algorithms that make a series of locally optimal choices in the hopes of finding a globally optimal solution. In this chapter, we'll explore when and why to use greedy algorithms, discuss real-world examples like the **activity selection** and **coin change** problems, and provide coding examples to implement greedy solutions.

When and Why to Use Greedy Algorithms

1. **What is a Greedy Algorithm?**

   o A greedy algorithm builds up a solution by repeatedly making the choice that looks best at each step (i.e., the choice that seems most beneficial at the moment).

   o It doesn't look at the overall structure of the problem but instead focuses on making locally optimal decisions, aiming to reach an overall optimal solution.

2. **Characteristics of Greedy Algorithms**

   o **Greedy Choice Property**: A globally optimal solution can be achieved by choosing the locally optimal option at each step.

   o **Optimal Substructure**: An optimal solution to the problem can be constructed from optimal solutions to its subproblems.

3. **When to Use Greedy Algorithms**

   o Greedy algorithms are typically efficient and work best for problems where the greedy choice property and optimal substructure hold.

   o They are often simpler and faster than dynamic programming or exhaustive search, making them ideal when an optimal solution can be found by making a series of local optimizations.

4. **Limitations of Greedy Algorithms**

o Greedy algorithms don't always yield optimal solutions, particularly when the problem lacks the greedy choice property.

o They work well for specific types of problems but may fail to find the best solution in cases where later choices affect earlier ones.

Real-World Examples

1. **Activity Selection Problem**
   o **Problem**: Given a list of activities with start and end times, find the maximum number of activities that can be scheduled without overlapping.
   o **Greedy Approach**: Sort activities by their end times. Select each activity that starts after the last selected activity has finished.
   o **Reasoning**: Choosing activities with the earliest finish times maximizes the time left for future activities, enabling the maximum number of non-overlapping activities.

Python Code for Activity Selection:

```python
def activity_selection(activities):
    # Sort activities by their end times
    activities.sort(key=lambda x: x[1])
```

```
selected_activities = [activities[0]]
last_end_time = activities[0][1]

for i in range(1, len(activities)):
    if activities[i][0] >= last_end_time:
        selected_activities.append(activities[i])
        last_end_time = activities[i][1]

return selected_activities

# Example usage
activities = [(1, 4), (3, 5), (0, 6), (5, 7), (3, 8), (5, 9), (6, 10),
(8, 11), (8, 12), (2, 13), (12, 14)]
selected = activity_selection(activities)
print("Selected activities:", selected)   # Outputs: Selected
activities that maximize the count
```

Explanation:

- The activities are sorted by their end times, allowing us to select non-overlapping activities by choosing the earliest finishing ones.
- This greedy choice of the earliest finish time allows us to maximize the number of activities.

2. **Coin Change Problem (Greedy Solution for Specific Coin Systems)**

o **Problem**: Given a set of coin denominations and an amount, find the minimum number of coins needed to make the amount.

o **Greedy Approach**: Always choose the largest denomination coin that doesn't exceed the remaining amount.

o **Limitation**: This approach works optimally only if the coin denominations are canonical (e.g., U.S. coin system). For other coin sets, dynamic programming is usually required for an optimal solution.

Python Code for Coin Change (Greedy):

python
```python
def coin_change(coins, amount):
    coins.sort(reverse=True)   # Sort coins in descending order
    num_coins = 0
    for coin in coins:
        if amount == 0:
            break
        count = amount // coin
        num_coins += count
        amount -= coin * count
```

return num_coins if amount == 0 else -1 # Return -1 if change is not possible

```
# Example usage
coins = [25, 10, 5, 1]
amount = 63
print("Minimum coins required:", coin_change(coins, amount))  # Outputs: Minimum number of coins for 63 cents
```

Explanation:

- o By always selecting the largest coin possible, we reduce the amount left to be made up quickly.
- o For standard coin systems, this approach minimizes the number of coins effectively. However, this solution may not work optimally with arbitrary coin denominations.

3. **Fractional Knapsack Problem**
   - o **Problem**: Given a set of items, each with a weight and value, and a maximum weight capacity, determine the maximum value that can be achieved. Items can be divided into fractions.
   - o **Greedy Approach**: Calculate the value-to-weight ratio for each item, sort items by this ratio in descending order, and take as much of each item as possible until the knapsack is full.

o **Reasoning**: By selecting items with the highest value per unit weight, the total value is maximized.

Python Code for Fractional Knapsack:

python

```python
def fractional_knapsack(items, capacity):
    # Sort items by value-to-weight ratio in descending order
    items.sort(key=lambda x: x[1] / x[0], reverse=True)

    total_value = 0
    for weight, value in items:
        if capacity == 0:
            break
        # Take as much of the item as possible
        take_weight = min(weight, capacity)
        total_value += (take_weight / weight) * value
        capacity -= take_weight

    return total_value

# Example usage
items = [(10, 60), (20, 100), (30, 120)]   # Each item is (weight, value)
capacity = 50
```

```python
print("Maximum value:", fractional_knapsack(items, capacity))  # Outputs: Maximum value that can be carried
```

Explanation:

- o By sorting items by value-to-weight ratio, we maximize the value per unit weight in the knapsack.
- o This approach works for fractional items, as we can take portions of each item as needed.

Coding Examples to Implement Greedy Solutions

1. **Huffman Coding (Greedy for Data Compression)**
   - o **Problem**: Given a set of characters and their frequencies, create a binary tree to assign variable-length codes to characters, minimizing the overall code length.
   - o **Greedy Approach**: Repeatedly combine the two least frequent nodes into a new node until only one node remains.

   Python Code for Huffman Coding:

```python
python
import heapq
from collections import defaultdict

class HuffmanNode:
```

```python
    def __init__(self, freq, char=None, left=None,
right=None):
        self.freq = freq
        self.char = char
        self.left = left
        self.right = right

    def __lt__(self, other):
        return self.freq < other.freq

def huffman_encoding(frequencies):
    # Create a priority queue (min-heap) from the character
frequencies
    heap = [HuffmanNode(freq, char) for char, freq in
frequencies.items()]
    heapq.heapify(heap)

    # Build the Huffman tree
    while len(heap) > 1:
        left = heapq.heappop(heap)
        right = heapq.heappop(heap)
        merged = HuffmanNode(left.freq + right.freq,
left=left, right=right)
        heapq.heappush(heap, merged)
```

```python
# Generate Huffman codes from the tree
root = heap[0]
codes = {}
def generate_codes(node, current_code=""):
    if node.char is not None:
        codes[node.char] = current_code
        return
    generate_codes(node.left, current_code + "0")
    generate_codes(node.right, current_code + "1")

generate_codes(root)
return codes


# Example usage
frequencies = {'a': 5, 'b': 9, 'c': 12, 'd': 13, 'e': 16, 'f': 45}
codes = huffman_encoding(frequencies)
print("Huffman Codes:", codes)
```

Explanation:

- Huffman coding uses a greedy approach to build a tree where the most frequent characters have shorter codes, minimizing the overall size of encoded data.

In this chapter, we explored greedy algorithms, which build solutions by making locally optimal choices at each step. We discussed when greedy algorithms are appropriate, covered real-world examples (like **activity selection**, **coin change**, and **fractional knapsack**), and implemented solutions in Python. Greedy algorithms are efficient and straightforward but work best in problems where local optimality leads to a global optimum.

In the next chapter, we'll move on to **advanced graph algorithms**, covering algorithms like Prim's and Kruskal's for finding minimum spanning trees and understanding their applications.

CHAPTER 21: ADVANCED DATA STRUCTURES - TRIES AND SEGMENT TREES

Advanced data structures like **tries** and **segment trees** provide specialized solutions for efficient data processing. This chapter introduces these structures, explains how to implement tries for efficient text searching, and explores real-world applications like autocompletion.

Introduction to Advanced Data Structures

1. **Why Use Advanced Data Structures?**
   - Basic data structures (arrays, linked lists, trees) are often efficient but may not be optimized for specialized tasks.
   - Advanced data structures like tries and segment trees are tailored for problems that require specific functionalities, such as fast prefix searches or range queries.

2. **Applications of Tries and Segment Trees**
   - **Tries**: Commonly used for tasks involving prefixes, like searching, autocompletion, and spell-checking.
   - **Segment Trees**: Useful for range queries on arrays, such as finding sums, minimums, or maximums within subarrays.

Implementing Tries for Efficient Text Searching

1. **What is a Trie?**
   - A **trie** (or prefix tree) is a tree-like data structure where each node represents a character. It efficiently handles prefixes by sharing common parts of strings.

- o **Root Node**: Represents the beginning of all stored strings.
- o **Children Nodes**: Each child represents a character in the string.
- o **End of Word Marker**: Typically, a boolean flag at the end of a word to mark that a complete word ends at this node.

2. **Operations on Tries**

- o **Insertion**: Add each character of a word as a node. If a character exists, move to the next node; otherwise, create a new node.
- o **Search**: Traverse nodes character by character to find words or prefixes.
- o **Deletion**: (Optional) Remove nodes, ensuring not to affect shared paths between prefixes.

3. **Python Code for Trie Implementation**

Trie Node and Trie Class:

python
```
class TrieNode:
    def __init__(self):
        self.children = {}
        self.is_end_of_word = False


class Trie:
```

```python
def __init__(self):
    self.root = TrieNode()

def insert(self, word):
    node = self.root
    for char in word:
        if char not in node.children:
            node.children[char] = TrieNode()
        node = node.children[char]
    node.is_end_of_word = True

def search(self, word):
    node = self.root
    for char in word:
        if char not in node.children:
            return False
        node = node.children[char]
    return node.is_end_of_word

def starts_with(self, prefix):
    node = self.root
    for char in prefix:
        if char not in node.children:
            return False
        node = node.children[char]
```

```
        return True
```

Explanation:

- insert(word): Adds each character of the word as a node, creating a new node only if the character is not already present.
- search(word): Checks if the word is present by traversing nodes. Returns True if it reaches a node marked as the end of the word.
- starts_with(prefix): Checks if any words in the trie start with the given prefix.

Example Usage:

```python
python
trie = Trie()
trie.insert("hello")
trie.insert("help")
trie.insert("helium")

print("Search 'hello':", trie.search("hello"))  # Outputs: True
print("Search 'hero':", trie.search("hero"))     # Outputs: False
print("Starts with 'he':", trie.starts_with("he"))  # Outputs: True
```

4. **Real-World Application: Autocompletion**

- Autocompletion systems use tries to efficiently find all words starting with a given prefix. For instance, typing "hel" may suggest "hello," "help," and "helium" as completions.

- **Autocomplete Implementation**: To find all words starting with a prefix, modify the starts_with function to traverse the trie from the prefix node and collect all possible words.

Python Code for Autocompletion:

```python
class TrieWithAutocomplete(Trie):
    def autocomplete(self, prefix):
        def dfs(node, prefix, results):
            if node.is_end_of_word:
                results.append(prefix)
            for char, next_node in node.children.items():
                dfs(next_node, prefix + char, results)

        results = []
        node = self.root
        for char in prefix:
            if char not in node.children:
                return results
            node = node.children[char]
```

```
dfs(node, prefix, results)
return results


# Example usage
trie = TrieWithAutocomplete()
trie.insert("hello")
trie.insert("help")
trie.insert("helium")
trie.insert("hero")


print("Autocomplete 'he':", trie.autocomplete("he"))    #
Outputs: ['hello', 'help', 'helium', 'hero']
```

Explanation:

o autocomplete(prefix): Uses a depth-first search (DFS) to collect all words that start with the given prefix.

Segment Trees for Efficient Range Queries

1. **What is a Segment Tree?**

   o A **segment tree** is a binary tree used to perform range queries and updates efficiently. Each node represents a range or segment of the array and stores information (like sum or minimum) about that range.

o Segment trees allow range queries (e.g., sum of elements, minimum element) and updates in O(log n) time.

2. **Building a Segment Tree**

o A segment tree is usually implemented as an array. For an array of length n, the segment tree array can be of size 2 * 2^ceil(log2(n)) - 1 to store nodes representing ranges.

o Each node in the tree represents a segment, with the root representing the entire array, and each child node representing a sub-segment.

3. **Python Code for Segment Tree Implementation**

Segment Tree Class for Range Sum Queries:

python
```
class SegmentTree:
    def __init__(self, arr):
        self.n = len(arr)
        self.tree = [0] * (2 * self.n)
        # Build the segment tree
        for i in range(self.n):
            self.tree[self.n + i] = arr[i]
        for i in range(self.n - 1, 0, -1):
            self.tree[i] = self.tree[2 * i] + self.tree[2 * i + 1]
```

```python
def update(self, index, value):
    # Update a single element
    index += self.n
    self.tree[index] = value
    while index > 1:
        index //= 2
        self.tree[index] = self.tree[2 * index] + self.tree[2 * index + 1]

def range_sum(self, left, right):
    # Calculate sum in the range [left, right)
    left += self.n
    right += self.n
    total = 0
    while left < right:
        if left % 2 == 1:
            total += self.tree[left]
            left += 1
        if right % 2 == 1:
            right -= 1
            total += self.tree[right]
        left //= 2
        right //= 2
    return total
```

Explanation:

- o **Building the Tree**: Initialize leaf nodes with the array values, then calculate each parent node by summing its children.

- o **Updating the Tree**: Update a single element and adjust ancestor nodes to maintain correct segment sums.

- o **Range Sum Query**: Traverse segments based on whether each index is even or odd, summing up values in the specified range.

Example Usage:

python
Copy code

```python
arr = [1, 3, 5, 7, 9, 11]
seg_tree = SegmentTree(arr)

print("Range sum (1, 4):", seg_tree.range_sum(1, 4))   # Outputs: 15 (3 + 5 + 7)
seg_tree.update(2, 6)  # Update element at index 2 to 6
print("Range sum (1, 4) after update:", seg_tree.range_sum(1, 4))  # Outputs: 16 (3 + 6 + 7)
```

4. **Real-World Application: Range Queries and Updates**
   - o Segment trees are widely used in applications where we need efficient range queries and updates, such as:

- **Database management**: Maintaining aggregate statistics (e.g., sum, min, max) over specific rows or columns.
- **Financial analysis**: Quickly calculating sums or averages over selected periods in financial data.
- **Gaming**: Tracking data across regions, like player scores or health points within specific zones.

In this chapter, we introduced **tries** and **segment trees**, two advanced data structures that provide efficient solutions for specialized tasks. We implemented tries for fast prefix-based text searching and autocompletion, and segment trees for efficient range queries and updates. These structures offer significant performance improvements in applications involving string search, text processing, and range-based calculations.

In the next chapter, we'll explore **graph algorithms for shortest paths and cycles**, covering algorithms like Floyd-Warshall, Prim's, and Kruskal's, along with their practical applications.

CHAPTER 22: PROBLEM-SOLVING TECHNIQUES AND INTERVIEW TIPS

Developing strong problem-solving skills is essential for both coding interviews and real-world programming challenges. This chapter covers a structured approach to tackling problems, offers practice problems that combine multiple data structures and algorithms, and shares practical tips for coding interviews.

Approaching Problems Step-by-Step

1. **Understand the Problem Thoroughly**

   o **Read the Problem Statement Carefully**: Take time to fully understand the problem. Misinterpreting the requirements is a common cause of errors.

   o **Clarify Constraints and Edge Cases**: Ask questions or re-read the statement to clarify any vague points. Think about constraints (e.g., input size, time complexity) and edge cases (e.g., empty inputs, maximum or minimum values).

2. **Identify the Input and Output**

   o Clearly define what inputs you receive and what outputs are expected. Knowing the exact format helps ensure your solution meets the requirements.

3. **Break Down the Problem into Smaller Parts**

   o **Identify Subproblems**: Many problems can be broken down into smaller, simpler problems that can be solved independently or recursively.

   o **Recognize Patterns**: Look for patterns, such as whether the problem requires sorting, searching, or dynamic programming.

4. **Choose the Right Data Structures and Algorithms**

   o Based on the identified patterns, select appropriate data structures and algorithms. For example:

     ▪ Use **hash tables** for quick lookups.

- Use **stacks or queues** for problems requiring order preservation.
- Apply **dynamic programming** for problems with overlapping subproblems.

5. **Plan Your Solution**

   o **Write Pseudocode**: Outline the solution step-by-step in pseudocode. This helps in organizing your thoughts and can reveal potential errors or inefficiencies.

   o **Evaluate Time and Space Complexity**: Before coding, analyze the time and space complexity to ensure the solution meets performance requirements.

6. **Implement the Solution**

   o Write clean and organized code, following the structure of your pseudocode. Focus on getting a working version first; you can optimize later if necessary.

7. **Test with Different Cases**

   o **Use Sample Inputs**: Test your solution with sample inputs, including edge cases, to ensure correctness.

   o **Optimize if Needed**: After confirming that the solution works, look for ways to optimize if the initial solution is too slow or uses excessive memory.

Practice Problems Combining Multiple Structures/Algorithms

Here are some problems that require using combinations of data structures and algorithms. Practicing these can strengthen your ability to solve complex problems efficiently.

1. **LRU Cache Implementation**
    - o **Problem**: Design a data structure that implements a Least Recently Used (LRU) cache, which evicts the least recently accessed item when the cache reaches its capacity.
    - o **Concepts Used**: **Hash Table** for quick lookups, **Doubly Linked List** to maintain the order of items.
    - o **Approach**: Use a hash table to map keys to nodes in a doubly linked list. The linked list maintains the order of access, allowing efficient removal of the least recently used item.

    Hint: Libraries like Python's OrderedDict can simplify this implementation.

2. **Word Ladder (Shortest Path in a Graph)**
    - o **Problem**: Given a start word, an end word, and a list of allowed transformations, find the shortest path (minimum transformations) from the start word to the end word.
    - o **Concepts Used**: **Graph Algorithms (BFS)**, **Trie** for efficient prefix matching.

o **Approach**: Treat each word as a node and each transformation as an edge. Use BFS to find the shortest path from the start word to the end word. Use a trie or hash set to efficiently store and look up words in the dictionary.

3. **Skyline Problem**

o **Problem**: Given a list of buildings (each represented by its starting and ending points and height), find the skyline formed by these buildings when viewed from a distance.

o **Concepts Used: Sorting, Priority Queue (Heap).**

o **Approach**: Sort the building edges (start and end points) by x-coordinates. Use a max-heap to keep track of building heights and update the skyline whenever the height changes.

4. **Minimum Window Substring**

o **Problem**: Given a string s and a target string t, find the minimum window in s that contains all characters of t.

o **Concepts Used: Sliding Window, Hash Map.**

o **Approach**: Use two pointers (sliding window) to keep track of the current window. Use a hash map to count occurrences of characters and adjust the window to find the smallest valid substring.

5. **Kth Largest Element in a Stream**

- o **Problem**: Design a data structure that maintains the kth largest element in a stream of integers.
- o **Concepts Used**: **Min-Heap**.
- o **Approach**: Use a min-heap of size k to keep the largest k elements in the stream, with the smallest element at the top.

Tips for Coding Interviews and Real-World Problem-Solving

1. **Communicate Clearly**
   - o Talk through your thought process during interviews. Explain why you're choosing certain approaches and data structures. Communication shows your analytical skills and helps the interviewer understand your reasoning.

2. **Be Mindful of Edge Cases**
   - o Ask about or consider edge cases, such as empty inputs, very large numbers, or unexpected data. Handling edge cases well demonstrates that you're thorough and pay attention to detail.

3. **Optimize Gradually**
   - o Start with a working solution, even if it's not the most efficient. Once you have a functional version, look for ways to optimize. In interviews, this shows a pragmatic approach to problem-solving.

4. **Prioritize Code Readability**

○ Write clean, modular code that's easy to understand. Use descriptive variable names, add comments, and break down complex logic into smaller functions. Readable code is easier to debug and review.

5. **Understand Complexity and Trade-offs**

○ Know the time and space complexities of common data structures and algorithms. This knowledge helps you make better decisions in choosing the right approach and justifying your solution.

6. **Prepare for Common Data Structures and Algorithms**

○ Be comfortable with common algorithms (sorting, searching, dynamic programming, graph traversal) and data structures (arrays, hash tables, trees, stacks, queues). Many interview questions are variations of these basics.

7. **Practice Mock Interviews**

○ Simulate real interview conditions by timing yourself and practicing with a friend or online platform. Mock interviews build confidence and help you refine your problem-solving approach.

8. **Stay Calm and Be Open to Hints**

○ If you're stuck, stay calm and ask clarifying questions. Interviewers often provide hints, so be receptive and incorporate feedback.

Example: Solving an Interview Problem Step-by-Step

Problem: Given a binary tree, find the lowest common ancestor (LCA) of two nodes.

1. **Clarify the Problem**
   - Confirm if it's a binary search tree (BST) or a general binary tree (this affects the approach). Ask if node values are unique and if both nodes are guaranteed to exist in the tree.

2. **Identify Key Concepts**
   - This problem involves **tree traversal** and finding a common ancestor. If it's a BST, we can use the properties of BSTs to find the LCA more easily.

3. **Choose an Approach**
   - For a binary tree, we can use **recursion** to traverse the tree. If we find one of the nodes in the left subtree and the other in the right, the current node is the LCA.

4. **Write Pseudocode**

python
```python
def find_lca(root, node1, node2):
    if not root or root == node1 or root == node2:
        return root
    left = find_lca(root.left, node1, node2)
    right = find_lca(root.right, node1, node2)
    if left and right:
```

```
return root
```

```
return left if left else right
```

5. **Analyze Complexity**
   o **Time Complexity**: $O(n)$, where n is the number of nodes, as each node is visited once.
   o **Space Complexity**: $O(h)$, where h is the height of the tree, due to the recursion stack.

6. **Code the Solution and Test**
   o Implement the solution in code, test with a sample binary tree, and check various cases, such as both nodes being in the same subtree or the tree having only one node.

In this final chapter, we discussed effective problem-solving techniques, covering a structured approach to understanding and solving problems. We explored practice problems combining multiple structures and algorithms, and shared tips for excelling in coding interviews. With the skills you've developed throughout this book, you're equipped to tackle both interview questions and real-world challenges.

As a next step, consider practicing on online coding platforms, engaging in mock interviews, and exploring advanced algorithms to further solidify your knowledge and problem-solving abilities.

CHAPTER 23: EXPLORING ADVANCED TOPICS IN DATA STRUCTURES AND ALGORITHMS

In this final chapter, we delve into some advanced topics in data structures and algorithms. These concepts build upon the foundational knowledge covered in the previous chapters, introducing new methods for handling even more complex programming challenges. The topics covered here are particularly useful for solving high-level problems in fields like artificial intelligence, machine learning, computational biology, and competitive programming. This chapter provides insights into areas that will enhance your problem-solving toolkit and prepare you for tackling specialized problems in advanced software development and research.

Advanced Topics Covered in This Chapter

1. **Balanced Binary Search Trees** (AVL Trees, Red-Black Trees)
   - An overview of self-balancing binary search trees.
   - Implementing AVL Trees and understanding the rotations for balancing.
   - Real-world applications, such as maintaining ordered data in databases.

2. **Suffix Trees and Suffix Arrays**
   - Explanation of suffix trees and suffix arrays for fast substring matching.
   - Building a suffix array for efficient text processing tasks.
   - Applications in bioinformatics (DNA sequence matching) and text processing.

3. **Fenwick Trees (Binary Indexed Trees)**
   - Introduction to Fenwick trees and their efficiency in range queries.
   - Implementing Fenwick trees for cumulative frequency tables.
   - Applications in competitive programming for range sum and update queries.

4. **Advanced Graph Algorithms**

   o Overview of advanced graph algorithms for pathfinding and cycle detection.

   o Algorithms like Tarjan's for finding strongly connected components.

   o Floyd-Warshall for all-pairs shortest paths and detecting negative cycles.

5. **Disjoint Set Union (Union-Find)**

   o Explanation of union-find data structures for managing sets.

   o Implementation with path compression and union by rank.

   o Applications in network connectivity, clustering, and Kruskal's algorithm.

6. **Approximation Algorithms**

   o Introduction to algorithms that provide near-optimal solutions.

   o Greedy and heuristic approaches for NP-hard problems like traveling salesman.

   o Applications in fields where exact solutions are impractical.

1. Balanced Binary Search Trees (AVL Trees, Red-Black Trees)

Balanced binary search trees (BBSTs) are essential for maintaining ordered data with efficient search, insertion, and deletion operations. Unlike standard binary search trees, BBSTs maintain a balanced structure, ensuring that the height remains approximately O(log n), which prevents degeneration into a linked list.

- **AVL Trees**:
    - AVL trees are self-balancing binary search trees where the heights of the left and right subtrees of any node differ by at most one.
    - Rotations (single or double) are used to restore balance after an insertion or deletion.
    - **Implementation**: Code examples for single and double rotations and insertion with balancing.
- **Red-Black Trees**:
    - Red-black trees are a type of balanced BST where each node is colored either red or black, following specific rules to maintain balance.
    - Used in many standard libraries (e.g., Java's TreeMap) due to their efficiency in dynamic set operations.

Applications:

- BBSTs are used in databases and file systems where dynamic ordered data management is required.

2. Suffix Trees and Suffix Arrays

Suffix trees and suffix arrays are powerful data structures for handling text-based operations efficiently, such as substring search and longest common prefix calculations.

- **Suffix Trees**:
    - o A suffix tree is a compressed trie of all suffixes of a given string, allowing efficient substring matching.
    - o While complex to implement, it provides O(m) search time for a pattern of length m within a text.
- **Suffix Arrays**:
    - o Suffix arrays are a space-efficient alternative to suffix trees and are easier to construct.
    - o Often paired with a longest common prefix (LCP) array for advanced text processing tasks.

Applications:

- o Used in bioinformatics (e.g., DNA sequence matching) and search engines for pattern matching within large texts.

3. Fenwick Trees (Binary Indexed Trees)

Fenwick trees, also known as binary indexed trees, are data structures that support efficient prefix sum queries and updates.

- **Functionality**:

- o They allow you to perform both point updates and prefix sum queries in O(log n) time.
- o Useful in situations where frequent updates and queries on cumulative data are required.

- **Implementation**:
  - o Explanation of how to construct, update, and query a Fenwick tree using bitwise operations.
  - o Demonstrating applications in scenarios like frequency tables and dynamic prefix sums.

Applications:

- o Commonly used in competitive programming and statistical data analysis.

4. Advanced Graph Algorithms

Advanced graph algorithms extend the basic traversal and shortest path algorithms to solve more complex problems.

- **Tarjan's Algorithm**:
  - o Used for finding strongly connected components in directed graphs.
  - o Essential in understanding the structure of networks and determining component connectivity.
- **Floyd-Warshall Algorithm**:
  - o An all-pairs shortest path algorithm that can also detect negative cycles.

o Provides insights into graph theory and is useful for understanding distances between all nodes in a network.

Applications:

o Network routing, web link analysis, and circuit design.

5. Disjoint Set Union (Union-Find)

The union-find or disjoint set union (DSU) data structure is efficient for managing and merging disjoint sets, making it useful for connectivity-related problems.

- **Implementation**:
  - o Code for union by rank and path compression, optimizing for efficient union and find operations.
  - o Explanation of the amortized time complexity, which is nearly constant for most operations.
- **Applications**:
  - o Used in clustering, Kruskal's minimum spanning tree algorithm, and network connectivity problems.

6. Approximation Algorithms

For many NP-hard problems, finding an exact solution is computationally infeasible. Approximation algorithms provide feasible solutions within an acceptable error margin.

- **Greedy and Heuristic Approaches**:
  - ○ Introduction to approximation algorithms for problems like the traveling salesman and knapsack.
  - ○ Explanation of algorithms that find approximate solutions in polynomial time.
- **Applications**:
  - ○ Used in resource allocation, network design, and scheduling tasks where perfect solutions are impractical.

Practical Tips for Tackling Advanced Problems

As you approach these advanced data structures and algorithms, remember that these topics are intended to be used for complex and high-performance applications. Here are some tips to effectively tackle these advanced topics:

1. **Break Down Complexity**: For each advanced topic, start by understanding the underlying principles and simple use cases before moving to full implementations.
2. **Leverage Libraries When Possible**: Many advanced data structures have been implemented and optimized in various libraries. For production-grade applications, consider using these libraries unless custom solutions are necessary.
3. **Practice with Real-World Problems**: Advanced topics are best learned through practical applications. Practice with

real-world problems from competitive programming platforms to solidify your understanding.

4. **Visualize the Process**: For complex structures like suffix trees or red-black trees, visualization tools and step-by-step diagrams can help clarify each step of the algorithm.

5. **Focus on Optimizations**: Understand why specific optimizations (e.g., path compression in union-find, rotations in AVL trees) are applied. This knowledge will help you tailor algorithms to unique scenarios.

Final Words: Becoming a Well-Rounded Problem Solver

With this final chapter, you have reached the culmination of an in-depth journey through data structures and algorithms. Mastery of these topics not only prepares you for complex programming challenges but also equips you with the ability to adapt and innovate solutions to real-world problems.

As you move forward, continue exploring, experimenting, and building. Data structures and algorithms are tools that grow more valuable with practice, and the more you apply them, the better you'll understand their power. Advanced topics provide endless avenues for specialization, so whether you pursue a career in software development, research, or data science, you now have the foundation to tackle even the most challenging problems.

Congratulations on completing "Practical Guide to Data Structures and Algorithms in Python." The journey of a software engineer and problem solver is ongoing—each new challenge is an opportunity to deepen your understanding and refine your skills.

ADDITIONAL TIPS FOR USING THIS BOOK EFFECTIVELY

This book is designed with a hands-on, practice-oriented approach to learning data structures and algorithms. As you work through each chapter, you'll find the following features to help reinforce your understanding and build your coding skills:

1. Code Examples: Bringing Concepts to Life with Python

Each chapter is filled with real-world Python code snippets that illustrate the data structures and algorithms discussed. These code examples aren't just abstract examples—they're designed to be practical and relevant, showcasing how these concepts apply to actual programming challenges.

The Python code provided in each chapter:

- **Follows Best Practices**: We use clean, readable syntax, clear variable names, and comments to enhance understanding.
- **Includes Edge Cases**: Where appropriate, the code examples address edge cases and explain how to handle them, helping you write resilient code.
- **Builds in Complexity**: Code snippets start with the basics and evolve to tackle more complex scenarios, giving you insight into how to enhance and adapt solutions.

To get the most out of these examples:

- **Type Out the Code**: Typing the code examples yourself helps you internalize the syntax and logic.
- **Experiment**: Modify parameters or test with different inputs to see how the code behaves. This experimentation will deepen your understanding.
- **Debug and Tweak**: Don't hesitate to debug or change parts of the code to better understand each component.

2. Problem Sets: Practice Makes Perfect

At the end of each chapter, you'll find problem sets with exercises tailored to the chapter's content. These problem sets range from straightforward questions to more complex challenges, ensuring a well-rounded practice experience. Each problem set is crafted to help you:

- **Apply What You Learned**: By solving problems right after studying the material, you can reinforce new concepts and cement your understanding.
- **Think Critically**: Many problems will require more than simply implementing what you've learned; they'll push you to adapt or combine concepts.
- **Develop Problem-Solving Skills**: Through practice, you'll build up a toolkit of coding patterns and techniques that will serve you well in both technical interviews and real-world projects.

Problem sets are designed with different levels of difficulty:

- **Easy**: Basic exercises to get you comfortable with the syntax and the algorithm.
- **Medium**: Problems that might require two or more steps, such as combining different data structures or adjusting your approach to handle edge cases.
- **Hard**: Complex problems that may require creativity and the combination of multiple concepts or algorithms.

These exercises provide a balanced mix of questions to ensure that you're building a strong foundation as you progress.

3. Visual Aids: Diagrams and Flowcharts for Clarity

Data structures and algorithms can sometimes be difficult to visualize. To help you understand complex concepts, this book includes visual aids such as:

- **Diagrams of Data Structures**: For topics like trees, graphs, heaps, and linked lists, diagrams show you the structure and relationships between elements, making it easier to understand traversal, insertion, deletion, and other operations.
- **Flowcharts for Algorithms**: Flowcharts are used to illustrate the step-by-step logic behind algorithms like sorting, searching, recursion, and dynamic programming.
- **Example Walkthroughs**: Visual aids are included to walk you through code examples line-by-line, showing how data moves through each function and how results are calculated at each stage.

Visual aids are especially useful for:

- **Understanding Recursive Algorithms**: Flowcharts and diagrams show how recursion unfolds step-by-step, making it easier to grasp the progression and termination of recursive calls.

- **Learning Tree and Graph Structures**: Trees and graphs are visual by nature, and diagrams help clarify concepts like traversal, balancing, and node relationships.
- **Following Sorting and Searching Algorithms**: Visual aids show how data is rearranged or compared, providing insight into the mechanics of algorithms like merge sort, quicksort, and binary search.

Tips for Getting the Most Out of Each Chapter

To maximize your learning and retention as you work through this book, here are some additional tips:

1. **Tackle Each Section at Your Own Pace**: Take time with each section to ensure full comprehension before moving on. If you find certain concepts challenging, revisit them before continuing to more advanced topics.
2. **Collaborate or Seek Peer Feedback**: Discussing problems or code with others can expose you to different problem-solving approaches and reinforce your own understanding. Online coding forums or study groups can be valuable for gaining feedback and sharing insights.
3. **Summarize Key Points**: After each chapter, jot down a summary of the most important concepts, algorithms, and techniques covered. Writing a brief summary in your own words is a great way to reinforce learning.

4. **Use Online Resources for Further Practice**: Many coding platforms, like LeetCode, HackerRank, and CodeSignal, offer problems similar to those discussed in this book. Practicing on these platforms is excellent preparation for real-world problem-solving and technical interviews.

5. **Reflect on Your Progress**: As you reach milestones or finish chapters, take a moment to review your progress. Reflecting on how your skills have grown will boost confidence and motivate you to tackle more complex challenges.

Why This Approach Will Make You a Better Programmer

The combination of real-world code examples, problem sets, and visual aids is designed to make you not just proficient but confident in using data structures and algorithms. This approach will help you:

- **Build Intuition**: The exercises and practical applications reinforce an intuitive understanding of each concept, so you'll know which data structures or algorithms to apply without second-guessing.

- **Prepare for Interviews**: Coding interviews test your ability to understand and implement solutions under pressure. This book's problem sets and interview tips provide targeted preparation to help you succeed in these high-stakes scenarios.

- **Think Critically and Adapt Solutions**: Real-world programming requires flexibility and problem-solving skills. By practicing the techniques in this book, you'll develop the adaptability needed to approach unfamiliar challenges with confidence.

Moving Forward

Mastering data structures and algorithms is an ongoing journey that offers continuous rewards. As you work through each chapter, build up your understanding, and tackle increasingly complex problems, you'll discover that these skills don't just improve your programming abilities—they'll transform the way you approach problem-solving in general.

With every chapter, you'll gain not only knowledge but practical expertise that you can apply in a variety of coding environments, from academic settings to professional software development. This book is designed to grow with you, providing both foundational knowledge and advanced techniques that will serve you throughout your coding career.

www.ingramcontent.com/pod-product-compliance
Lightning Source LLC
LaVergne TN
LVHW051325050326
832903LV00031B/3364